The Long Trip Home

A South American and Caribbean Adventure through the Past

BRIAN D. WYLLIE

iUniverse, Inc.

New York   Bloomington

The Long Trip Home
A South American and Caribbean Adventure through the Past

iUniverse books may be ordered through booksellers or by contacting:

iUniverse
1663 Liberty Drive
Bloomington, IN 47403
www.iuniverse.com
1-800-Authors (1-800-288-4677)

ISBN: 978-0-595-52972-8 (sc)
ISBN: 978-0-595-63025-7 (ebook)

Printed in the United States of America

iUniverse rev. date: 01/12/09

Dedication

I wrote this book during my wonderful wife Linda's two-year fight against first breast cancer and then two later battles with brain cancer. She lost her fight but always encouraged me to finally put my story on paper. We had planned to travel to Brasil and other locations I visited on my trip, but she only went to several of the islands in the Caribbean. She felt like she knew these places from hearing about them for thirty-four years, but I regret that she never got there. I dedicate this book to her, to all the wonderful trips that we did take together, and to the memories those trips created. I will continue to travel and take her with me in spirit.

Brian Wyllie, her loving husband.

Introduction

Someone once told me that everyone has a story—it just needs to be told. It's been over thirty-seven years now, and this story has had time to sift through my mind, get distorted by my memory, and make itself ready to come out.

I was a product of the sixties, one of the so-called "baby boomers." After rattling around in college for four years, trying to figure out what I wanted to be and what I wanted to do when I grew up, I joined the Peace Corps and shipped out to Brasil. The recruiters for the Peace Corps had been on the West Virginia University campus, trying to recruit some newly minted college graduates before the draft boards snatched them up. The idea of serving my country for two years and helping people better their standard of living appealed to me a lot more than improving my marksmanship. With my degree in economics, I fit well into a program for establishing fishing cooperatives in Brasil. I had little opportunity to travel up to this point in my life, and the lure of South America was the motivation for me to sign up. I spent two years in Brasil and returned to the United States in the fall of 1971. What follows is the story of that circuitous trip through much of South America and the islands of the Caribbean. Some names have been changed, as they say, "to protect the innocent," but as best as I can recall this is how it happened.

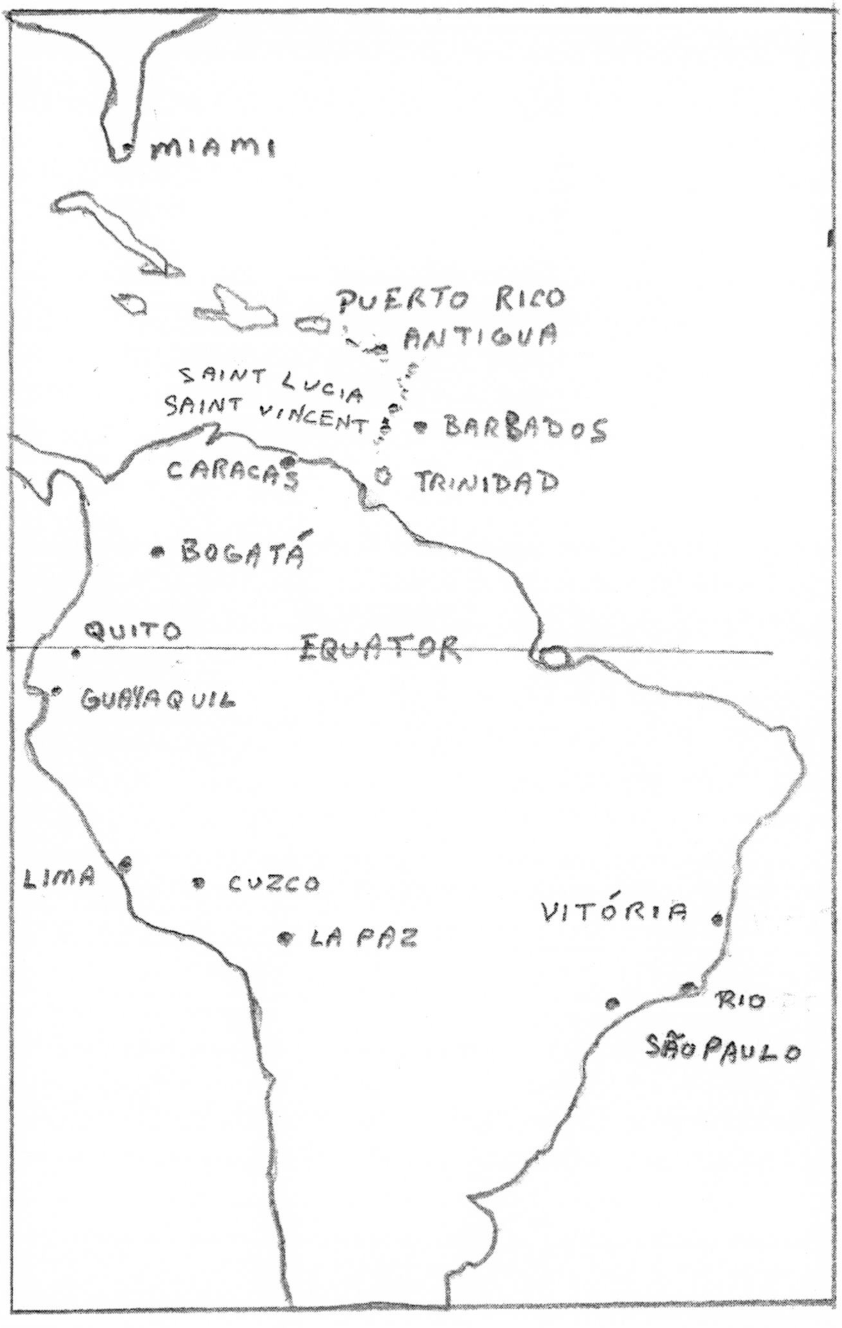
MIAMI
PUERTO RICO
ANTIGUA
SAINT LUCIA
SAINT VINCENT
BARBADOS
CARACAS
TRINIDAD
BOGATÁ
QUITO
EQUATOR
GUAYAQUIL
LIMA
CUZCO
LA PAZ
VITÓRIA
RIO
SÃO PAULO

Prologue

She was a kind of mousy-looking young woman, not much over five feet tall, and she seemed to be in a new uniform. Of all of the many customs officers at the airport in San Juan, Puerto Rico, she was the one I was sent to. I had been waiting in line with all the other passengers that had gotten off the plane from Antigua, and this was going to be my reentry into the United States as a citizen. When my turn came, I put the big leather duffle bag I had been carrying with me for three months on the table in front of the customs officer. I handed her my semi-diplomatic passport with a big smile. She looked at me in my basically unwashed condition and wearing clothes that had been on my back for most of the trip. Instead of taking pity on my battle-scarred bag and me, she calmly said, "Empty the bag on the table, sir."

I looked at her in shock and replied, "You have got to be kidding me. You don't want to know what is in this bag."

She replied, "Oh, on the contrary. I do want to know what is in that bag." I started to slowly pull things out of my three-foot-high leather bag and spread them out all over her table. Dirty underwear, pants, shirts, and sweatshirts, which I had been carrying the whole trip in all kinds of weather. I had been unable to wash clothes due to a lack of facilities. As the pile grew and the smell got a bit much, I was wondering, will she make me take every single thing from the bag?

She just kept looking at me and motioning for me to empty it, empty it. My concern grew as I continued to pull out muddy shoes, filthy socks, and all kinds of things that had accumulated in the lower regions of the bag. I slowly worked toward the bottom. What I was hoping was that I wouldn't have to empty out the last remaining items in the bag. The last two rolls of filthy socks contained a switchblade knife and a disassembled twenty-two-caliber pistol!

I was almost to the bottom but she kept saying, "Keep going."

I asked her one more time, "Do you really want any more of this junk on your table?" and waited for her answer.

Chapter 1: Brasil

9/5/71

Hi folks,

Well, as you can see, I didn't die or anything. I have just been lax in writing. In the last week or so, I've been to Vitória about five times and the rest of the time I've spent in the house. We have had heavy rain, exactly like you encountered last year. This winter was really nice with only about ten days of rain. The streak of good luck ran out suddenly and we have had downpours with drizzle in between, except it is not as cold.

I've also been busy selling all my stuff. Since the Peace Corps will only pay to ship thirty-six pounds of personal belongings back to the United States, I've been trying to sell almost all of my things. I don't want my bag to be too heavy, and I want to save room in it for anything that I might want to buy on the trip.

The local kids, and especially the guys my age, have a great interest in all things American. Blue jeans and other clothing made in the United States are not readily available in Brasil. They can be purchased in the big cities like Rio de Janeiro, but the cost is prohibitive. I have had no trouble

1

selling almost everything and have in fact had a tough time keeping enough clothing to get me through the trip! The locals also snapped up all my furniture, tape player, cooking equipment, and anything else that wasn't nailed down.

To my surprise, there has been no offer for the boat I built. I consequently gave it to the young guy who runs the daily operation at the cooperative. He has promised to continue allowing the local kids to borrow it to hunt for crayfish and crabs. The kids' mothers cook what they catch, and the seafood is then sold in the street for extra income.

I didn't want to write you a letter with my plans for my return trip until I got all the details straightened out. Due to the problems in Bolivia, I didn't know if I was still going there or not, etc. It now looks like the situation is better, so I'll be leaving Barra and going by bus and train from Rio to La Paz, Bolivia, on September twenty-first. I'll then go to Cuzco, Peru, and on to Machupicchu, the lost city of the Incas. From there I will fly to Lima, Peru, and then to Guayaquil, Ecuador. Next, I will try to travel by train over the Andes to Quito, Ecuador, on to Bogotá, Columbia, and then to Caracas, Venezuela. Finally, I will fly to Trinidad to start my inter-island trip to at least Puerto Rico before reaching Miami and the continental United States.

As this excerpt from my last letter home shows, I knew something about where I wanted to go but had no idea if I was going to make it or how the gaps in between the visits to cities would be filled. I was twenty-four years old at the time I wrote the letter and was itching to travel.

I had spent the previous two years as a Peace Corps volunteer. Our group was sent to Brasil to establish fishing cooperatives along the coast as well as at a few sites inland along rivers. Our project truly fit the old adage of, "Give them a fish, they will eat for a day. Teach them to fish, they will feed themselves for a lifetime." In our case, the fishermen knew how to fish better than we did. Our job was to show them better ways to market the fruits of their labor.

Prior to going to Brasil in 1969, our group assembled in Atlanta, Georgia. We were to train with four other Peace Corps groups. The others were going to establish electrical cooperatives, agricultural cooperatives, agricultural extension programs, and agricultural clubs in Brasil. We all needed a lot of cross-cultural training in order to work with the Brasilians on a person-to-person basis. We also, of course, needed a lot of language training if we were going to do any work at all! To accomplish all this training, a team of nearly thirty Brasilians from many areas of Brasil and at least a dozen bi-lingual Americans was assembled. We stayed in a hotel in downtown Atlanta, and we spent two weeks learning as much as we could about the culture of Brasil, especially the differences between our two cultures. If we were to work with the fishermen, we needed to know what actions might offend them, even if these things seemed trivial to us. By having Brasilians as teachers, we could ask questions and get first-hand knowledge of their way of living. Brasil is a huge country, and each region is quite different, just as in the United States where residents of New England have very different feelings about many subjects than residents of Atlanta, for example. It is no different in Brasil.

The Brasilians taught us as much as they could about their diversity as our short time together allowed. For at least half of each day, we would observe our new Brasilian friends act out scenarios and listen to their speech. In this way we were learning Portuguese the same way a child learns. We associated words with actions and heard the pronunciation as we would hear it in Brasil. Since our instructors came from all areas of Brasil, we were exposed to various accents as well. The dialogues, as they were referred to, were repeated many times each day and were added to with more complex scenarios as the days went by. Through repetition we started to memorize the dialogues even if we didn't know what all the words meant. At the end of this two-week learning experience, we were given a shocking announcement. We were to relocate to an old YMCA camp miles away from Atlanta, where, after a ceremony to bury the English language, we would be forbidden to utter one word of our native tongue! The philosophy behind this approach was that upon our arrival in Brasil, any problems that arose would have to be solved in Portuguese and not English. If we were dying and needed help, we would not be able to call timeout and speak English. No one spoke English where we were being assigned. I learned the wisdom of this way of thinking firsthand during the first few months I was in Brasil. I nearly died of dehydration, and it was necessary to telegraph our state director in the capitol and arrange transportation for me to a hospital there. This would not have been possible with basic freshman Portuguese.

The YMCA camp in Waco, Georgia, was Spartan to say the least. We were assigned to bunk houses, and I was lucky enough to get an upper bunk, closer to the Georgia heat of summer! After settling in, we were given a few days to acclimate to our new routine and then went through the dreaded ceremony. Total immersion into a foreign language is a painful process, but once you adjust it becomes a great learning experience. Our brains got accustomed to the sounds of the words, and we slowly built vocabulary. The main advantage to this method was that we only heard correctly spoken Portuguese, and it was delivered in a manner that we would encounter in Brasil. The month of training passed quickly. We had been given a taste of Brasilian culture, including many meals cooked the way we would encounter them. We also played soccer and other games that were mandatory to fitting into our new environment. The vocabularies for all these subjects were learned by experience and therefore better retained.

During our training period, both in Atlanta and Waco, we were repeatedly checked for health conditions and had any defects corrected. We were going to be sent to areas that did not necessarily have readily available health care. The government was spending a lot of money to train us and did not want us to have medical problems while in Brasil. Our teeth were checked out completely, and all necessary dental work was undertaken prior to our departure. In the area where I finally ended up working, the fishermen who had cavities solved the problem by having the offending tooth pulled! Dental work was done there, but the equipment was right out of the Marquis de Sade's closet, and the techniques came directly from his playbook. Fortunately for us, however, the Center for Disease Control (CDC) was located just outside Atlanta, and we were often taken there for care or personnel from the center came out to our camp. While we were training in Waco, most of our medical work was done on site since we were not to use or even hear English during this period. On one memorable occasion, a group of us had been playing soccer in the morning. After lunch we were treated to gigantic needles stuck into our rear ends and then sent to rest in our bunks. As you might recall, I had been given an upper bunk in our cabin. When called for dinner, I realized that I was effectively paralyzed from the waist down, and I fell out of my bunk! We were told that we were not to have done any exercise prior to receiving that particular injection. Playing soccer for several hours that morning had resulted in temporary paralysis.

By the end of our training in Georgia, we were all probably in the best physical shape of our lives. We had been given inoculations against every disease known to man and some that I think they invented just to give us more needles!

On September 15, 1969, we boarded a plane for Rio de Janeiro, Brasil. On a sad note here, several of the trainees were removed from the plane at the last minute. It seemed that their draft boards won the fight over the Peace Corps, which had just spent taxpayer money to train them. These were people with masters' degrees from Harvard and Yale who were going to set up businesses. Instead, they were now being sent to boot camp to fill a draft board quota for their state.

Our Varig jet was retrofitted to carry both passengers and cargo. Just behind the flight cabin there were a few bunks for the crew to take naps. The next section was filled with bags of rice and other goods from USAID for distribution in Brasil. Finally, in the rear of the plane, were our seats. If we got tired of sitting and wanted to sleep, we just went forward and slept on the rice bags! We stopped once in the Caribbean on Aruba and at Recife, Brasil, for fuel and finally arrived in Rio after more than twelve hours of travel. From Rio we traveled by ferry to Niterói. If one wished to make that trip today, a short drive over a new bridge is all it would take!

We only stayed a few days in Niterói, but one night a group of us decided to go back over to Rio to see some of the city. Since we had used the ferry to get to Niterói, we managed to do that part in reverse with no problems. Once in Rio, some of the best traveled of our small group managed to hail a cab, and we somehow got to one of the famous Rio beaches. At this point we realized that our month of Portuguese was not going to get us very far. As I recall there was a pizza shop where we could at least get something to eat. We walked around for a while and then, somehow, managed to find our way back to the hotel in Niterói.

Our next destination, after a few days of orientation in Niterói, was the seacoast town of Macaé. Our final month of in-country training took place there. Macaé is a lovely seacoast town in the state of Rio de Janeiro. It is large enough to have all the amenities for a comfortable life and yet small enough to not overwhelm. This was a perfect location for our group to get exposed to Brasilian culture. If we had stayed in Rio, for instance, I don't think that we would have gotten much of a feel for life in Brasil as it would be in the towns where we were to be assigned.

While in Macaé we had free time to explore the town. Since it was now spring in Brasil, there were tourists in Macaé. Word had spread that there were Americans staying in town, and several of the tourists would drop by the hotel to see what we were like. There was great interest in single, college-educated American males, and we had no trouble making friends with the locals! One cultural difference we soon learned was that the girls were very friendly, but they were always chaperoned by at least a sister if not a brother. The chaperone tried to disappear into the background as much as possible, but we knew that they were always there. The interaction was stimulating to say the least, but it proved to be most beneficial as a vocabulary builder and as a way to get us used to interacting with strangers in Portuguese. Since our stay was only going to be a brief one, no long-term relationships were a possibility. We spent the days learning a lot more of the language and as much as our instructors could tell us about the economy. My group's job was to establish a network of fishing cooperatives, so we needed to know how the fishermen were currently selling their catch in order to help them improve. We visited local fishermen and markets and observed the process of selling the catch firsthand. Once again vocabulary was a big issue, and these sessions helped us improve our ability to understand and discuss the subject of our work. After about a month of in-country training, we were deemed ready for the big test.

The final exam, so to speak, took the form of a do-or-die trip to a location given to us. We had to find transportation to our assigned town, rent living space for two weeks, and then return to Macaé. We were to observe the fishing community in the town and try to determine how the fishermen were selling their catch. This may not sound like too daunting a task, but try doing it all with only two months of training in a foreign language.

In 1969, we did not encounter any Brasilians who spoke English. I was sent to a small fishing village called Perocão in the next state north, which was called Espírito Santo. I rented a room in a house owned by the local bus driver's mother. I survived the two-week ordeal and returned to Macaé for my assignment.

I was assigned to a small coastal town, the one referred to in the letter home, called Barra do Itapemirim. Barra was only about an hour south of Perocão, and it was right on the beach where the Itapemirim River met the ocean. There was another town about a mile further south called Marataizes, and today the whole area is now referred to as Marataizes. A married couple, Marc and Linda, luckily joined me. Knowing that the three of us would be in the same location made our isolation much easier to deal with. We rented a small house together, and I lived with them for part of a year until I could find a house of my own in Marataizes. The Peace Corps expected us to live on a level close to that of the people we were sent to help, not like some embassy bureaucrat. Single volunteers got the same pay as married couples, and it was therefore quite difficult to find an affordable house on one salary. The Peace Corps originally wanted us to rent a room from a family and live with them, but I had done that for two weeks in Perocão and didn't want to do that for two years!

During that two-week stay in Perocão, I had my own room. In order to take a bath, I had to have a large galvanized tub filled with water and placed behind a curtain. The rest of the family went about their business while I bathed, and more than once some small child would wander past the curtain! I eventually bathed across the street at a bar where they had a showerhead above a toilet. In Brasil it was common practice to make the whole bathroom the shower stall. My bathrooms in Barra and Marataizes were set up that way also. I ate all my meals with the bus driver's family, and the menu took some getting used to. The chickens that ran around the house in the morning might be on your plate for dinner. The family was very pleased when I went out fishing one day and came home with a fine five-pound fish. I was forced to interact with the family at all levels, and that definitely benefited my study of the language.

I really missed my privacy, though, and vowed never to live under those conditions when I got my assignment.

I was finally able to rent a small house from one of the more prosperous fishermen in Marataizes. He had built the house next to his own house to rent out to tourists in the summer months. Since the house was vacant the rest of the year, I moved in for very little cost. When summer came around the next year, I was forced to move again and found a place on the second floor of an unfinished hotel. I had no electricity, water, or even a door, but I had a roof over my head and a mattress to sleep on. My little house beside the fisherman's was now renting for ten times what I had paid! By the end of that summer, Marc and Linda had been reassigned to another town further north, so I moved into the original house by myself. I now had the luxury of a two-bedroom house even if it cost me way too much.

We were given an allowance at the start of our service to buy necessary items like stoves, dishes, furniture, and so on. There were no refrigerators, so we just had to go shopping for food every day like the locals. I built a bed and other furniture for myself and Marc and Linda. I bought a stove and other essentials when I finally got my own house. To have a mattress for your bed, you had to order one. It was made for you out of straw and delivered in a few days. Our stoves were run on propane, and the gas tanks were replaced as they ran out. If you were unlucky enough to deplete your tank during the cooking of a meal, you usually had to wait until the next day to purchase a replacement. We could not afford to own back-up tanks.

Food was purchased daily at different locations. The butcher, for example, killed a steer every few days, and it was necessary to go to his shop and bargain for the cut of meat that you desired as he cut it from the animal. Marc, Linda, and I pooled our money and could often get the more expensive filet mignon. The meat, having just been cut, was not aged like we were accustomed to. We would have even the best cuts ground into hamburger. If the meat was ground, it was tasty and chewable. There was another butcher in town that only sold pork. He had a small refrigerator, so it was possible to purchase some cut of meat on almost any day. Marc and I worked with the fishermen every day, so we had access to fresh fish of all types. As a result we ate some variety of fish most days of the week. The fishermen caught all types of fish, including many sharks.

Shark meat is just like a giant scallop if it is cut across the grain and fried in butter. The best of all was the lobster, but that was their most valuable catch. Since the fishermen would almost never take payment from us, I went snorkeling for most of my lobster. There was a small island about one mile off the coast called Egg Island. It was called this because of its large seabird population. Diving the perimeter of this island yielded a never-ending supply of lobster. One of the primary reasons for building the boat mentioned in the letter home was to gain access to Egg Island. I grew up in a boat-building town on the Delaware River. My brother and I built our first boat when we were about ten years of age. It was built from a kit. To build a boat in Brasil I had to do everything from scratch. I went to a local lumber mill and had boards cut to the size I required from a log. The boat was nailed together with copper nails and caulked with string and tar. I converted it to a sailboat later and even made my own sail. My Brasilian friend's mother had a treadle sewing machine and she taught me how to sew with it. My wife was a great seamstress but she never sewed on a treadle machine. Shrimp was our biggest catch when it was in season. I knew that I was eating too much shrimp when I attempted to make cookies with shrimp instead of chocolate chips. We certainly tried to live somewhat on the level of the locals even if our ways of cooking and diets were a little different.

Also interesting was the number of vendors who wandered the streets each day. There was always a young boy on a horse with two five-gallon jugs of milk over his saddle. If you brought out a container he would ladle out whatever quantity of milk you needed that day. This method ensured that there was always milk on hand unless no one was at home when the boy arrived. The milk was straight from the cow and still warm, and we had to put the milk on the stove and bring it to a boil to pasteurize it. One of the volunteers to the south of us did not do this regularly and was sent home with tuberculosis.

I also had small loaves of bread delivered each morning and ate them with honey and margarine for breakfast. Butter spoiled quickly without refrigeration, but margarine kept well and was sold by weight on wax paper.

The farming area around Barra and Marataizes was known for pineapple production. When the fruits were in season, there were again small boys plying the streets with carts full of them. The boys knew where the Americans lived and would always stop by to try to sell as many pineapples to us as they could. We paid about five cents for each whole pineapple, but after about five or so our mouths were quite cut up and stinging. That quantity of pineapple is also very filling!

Other kids would stop by with trays of mussels their mothers had cooked. Some of the kids would borrow the boat that I used to go to Egg Island and go fishing. The kids would repay me with the giant land crabs and freshwater crayfish they caught. Both of these delicacies are a real treat.

Since Marc and I were out in the sun most of the day talking with the fishermen, we got dehydrated quite easily. Linda worked in the school system and consequently was not out in the sun as frequently. She also had access to drinking water whenever she was thirsty. During training the staff had drummed into us the idea that we should not drink any untreated water. As a result I tried to do with very little and only drank Coke or other bottled drinks during the day. The result of this foolish practice was that I developed a temperature of 105 degrees due to acute dehydration and had to spend several days recovering in a hospital. Upon my return, I purchased a large water filter. It was similar to a Brita filter. It consisted of a five-gallon clay pot with three filters on top of another five-gallon pot with a spigot. The top pot could be filled with water, which then passed down through the filters into the lower pot. As the water seeped through the pots, it evaporated and thus cooled the water. The spigot in the bottom pot, of course, supplied the now-potable water. From that time on, I never passed the filter in my house without having a drink. My adventure in a Brasilian hospital, at a time when my Portuguese was not so good, has kept me very aware of the potential for dehydration in warm climates. I could go on with my discussion of the lifestyle on the coast of Brasil, but it is time to get on with my trip back home to the United States.

My job was over. There was a functioning cooperative now run by the fishermen, and my two years of service were up. I traveled to Vitória, the capital of the state of Espírito Santo, where our state office was and completed the paperwork necessary to terminate my service. While in Vitória I met two Peace Corps volunteers, Steve and Sue, who had been in Bolivia until the recent revolution. The new government there no longer wanted Peace Corps volunteers in Bolivia, so they had had to leave. Now that the revolution was over, Steve and Sue were planning to return to the United States through Bolivia on much the same route that I had planned to take.

9/19/71

I finished my paperwork in Vitória and traveled by bus down to Rio to do my final checkout with Peace Corps before leaving the country. I ran into Steve and Sue again at the Florida Hotel. The Florida was the place to find volunteers if they were in Rio, as we all stayed there if we were in town for business. Any volunteers traveling from other countries would also stay there and could meet those of us who lived in Brasil. The volunteers could get great ideas of what to see and do on a budget that they could afford. Steve and Sue left for Bolivia on September twentieth, but I couldn't. I was having trouble cashing my termination check, and I needed the money to pay for my trip home.

As a volunteer in Brasil I was paid approximately one hundred dollars per month in cruzeiros. This currency has changed several times since I was there due to inflation, politics, and other factors; and the currency is now the real. During my period of service, we received several raises to adjust for inflation, but the raises were usually after the purchasing power of the cruzeiro had dropped quite a lot. From our salary we were expected to pay for lodging, food, and all expenses outside of medical and some travel. If we had to travel to Rio, for example, to negotiate contracts or deal with government paperwork, we were reimbursed for our bus tickets and hotel bill in Rio. When a volunteer finished their term of service, they received a termination check and a plane ticket to the nearest major U.S. airport to their former home address. In my case, it was a ticket to Philadelphia, worth about $380. I had somehow saved some money from my salary and needed to cash in the plane ticket to pay for my extended trip home. The bank in Rio finally cashed the check and I was funded.

9/21/71

With the money I got from the bank, I purchased an open ticket for several of the legs of my planned itinerary. I left Rio on the Viação Mato

11

Grosso bus line for Corumbá, at the border shared by Brasil and Bolivia. I was a day behind Steve and Sue, which was a hint of things to come. I just didn't know it yet.

In 1971, travel in the interior of Brasil was not like in the United States. One traveled on unimproved and unreliable dirt roads. We left Rio on what should have been about a fifteen-hour ride to Campo Grande. After nearly twenty hours of dusty, bone-jarring roads, the bearings on one of the bus wheels gave out. We were stranded on the side of the road about twenty-five kilometers from Campo Grande. The buses in Brasil at the time were usually very nicely appointed Mercedes models, and if you traveled on overnight trips they even had reclining seats that allowed for a somewhat decent sleep. Since the trip to Campo Grande was not an overnight venture, however, this bus was a standard model. Due to the mileage on mostly dirt roads that this bus had endured, it had seen a much rougher life than the buses between Rio and São Paulo, for instance.

Most of the passengers on the bus took this delay in stride and settled down to wait for the repairs to be made. I was on a mission to catch up with Steve and Sue, so I got off the bus with two Brasilians, and we were lucky enough to hitch a ride in a Dodge Dart to Campo Grande. If you think a twenty-hour ride over a dirt road in a Mercedes bus is rough, try chasing one in a Dodge Dart!

Unfortunately, we missed the bus out of Campo Grande by about forty minutes. Still on the chase, we decided to hire a car to pursue the bus ahead of us. After two hundred kilometers on a rough dirt road (we kept the windows open because there was no air conditioning in those days), we finally caught the bus at a rest stop in Aquiduana. The combination of the hitchhiking ride and the rented car left the three of us covered in dust and quite worn out, but we were way ahead of the poor souls on the first bus. They were probably still waiting for someone to arrive and replace the worn-out bearings.

The second bus wasn't much better than the first one. We spent fourteen more grueling hours, all on dirt roads. We also had to cross several rivers on wooden barges that could barely float a full-size Mercedes bus. When we arrived at the first river, I was wondering how we were going to get across. There was a post on our side, and I could see one on the other side as well. Between these posts was strung a cable with a wooden barge attached. Upon noticing the bus on the other side of the river, the barge operator started a small diesel engine. By passing the cable around a drum on the engine, he winched the barge over to our side of the river. Several planks were pulled out onto the bank, and the bus was driven very slowly and carefully onto the barge. There were barely a few feet on either side of the barge, and it was only six or eight feet longer than the bus as well. Luckily there was little current in the river as we crossed over and eventually reached the other side. The process of driving the bus over the planks was reversed at the opposite end of the barge to get on the shore. Had the bus tipped off the small barge due to current or waves, I doubt that many of the passengers would have gotten out before the bus sank. We encountered several other rivers that needed to be crossed and followed a similar procedure at each location. After these crossings, we headed west to Bolivia.

The bus's radiator kept overheating due to a leak, but we would just stop at streams and refill it. This method of dealing with a leaking radiator reminded me of the Jeep Rural that the Peace Corps office made available to the volunteers in Espírito Santo. If we needed to get to places that were not readily serviced by bus routes, we could request the Jeep. I rarely had the use of the Jeep since most of my traveling was to Rio or São Paulo or local. Brasil had excellent bus lines at the time since very few people had personal cars. Between the small coastal towns there was relatively good transportation, aside from the unpaved roads. Our local bus service on the beach was marginal and I usually used my bicycle, which was more reliable most of the time. On one of my trips in the Jeep, the radiator burst a freeze plug (like I really needed a freeze plug in Brasil), which promptly emptied the radiator. Luckily along the coast of Brasil there are many small streams and rivers, so I pulled over at nearly every one to refill the radiator and anything else in the Jeep that held water. I went from stream to stream until I finally made it to a gas station. I left the Jeep there for repairs and took a bus home. Several days later, I returned and retrieved the Jeep. We never went out on the road in the Jeep without a change of clothes and some food, even for a short trip. Any trip could wind up taking several days. We finally arrived in Corumba on the night of September twenty-second, and I got a room with one of the guys who had rented the chase car with me. I hoped that I could find Steve and Sue the next day.

9/23/71

I had to spend most of the day trying to get a visa for entry into Bolivia and then tickets for the only train into the country. There was only one place to purchase tickets in Corumbá, so my new Brasilian traveling partner and roommate Renato was with me when I got to the front of the line.

When I placed my American passport and newly obtained visa on the ticket counter, he said, "What is going on? You mean to tell me that you are not a Brasilian?" This was the best compliment I could have received. Not that being a Brasilian was bad, but through all we had just endured he was unable to detect that I was an American. This was like passing a final exam without knowing that I was taking one. During the two years I had spent in Brasil, I had assimilated well enough into the culture to pass as one of his countrymen. I had never thought to reveal that I was an American and had just told him that I was from Espírito Santo, which explained the difference in our accents. As I mentioned before, the accents in different parts of Brasil are as different as those from South Carolina and New York. I was able to talk with all the slang and idiomatic expressions that were in vogue at that time and had pulled off my transformation into a Brasilian quite well. As a side note, I had trouble assimilating back into the culture of the United States when I finally returned. I continued to use lots of Portuguese words and expressions that no one could understand.

In 1971 there were very few people crossing over into Bolivia by land as I was trying to do. With the recent revolution in Bolivia, the border crossing was a lot stricter than it might have been a few months earlier. The current Bolivian government was not as friendly toward the United States as the previous one had been, so a U.S. passport got a lot of scrutiny from the border officials. These guys were also new on the job, as they were replacing the officials that had worked for the previous government. I will just say that if one does not have to cross a border two weeks after a revolution, don't!

Luckily I found Steve and Sue, who had not yet been able to get a train heading west. I finally got all my papers in order, and we found out that a train would be leaving the next day for Santa Cruz, Bolivia. I was delighted to have reconnected with Steve and Sue since they were fluent in Spanish and familiar with Bolivia. We planned to spend at least a week in Bolivia, and I would now have a chance to see it in a much different light than I would have as just a tourist.

I spent the last night still sharing a room with my old traveling partner from the bus trip. I explained to him the change in my traveling plans, and he wished me good luck on the rest of my journey. He was only going as far as Santa Cruz, so we would have parted ways there anyway.

Chapter 2: Bolivia

9/24/71

We left Corumbá on a literina, which is a combination bus and train. The literina was about the size of a regular bus, but it ran on the train tracks instead of those horrible, rutted dirt roads crisscrossing Brasil. I had the privilege of sitting in the front seat beside the driver for the thirteen-hour trip. It was quite an experience. The literina did not stop for any reason except at stations and had a cowcatcher on the front to deal with anything that didn't get out of the way! During the crossing into Bolivia, we ran over, and I presume killed, two pigs, five birds, and one cow! It was quite interesting to see (I was right at the windshield) and feel the animals being killed as they passed under the train.

Along the way, the train would stop at various small towns. This was the only connection these towns had with the outside world since travel by land was too far and too harsh to be practical without a motorized vehicle of some kind. At each stop, many residents would present handmade crafts for sale. They would also hold up food items to the windows of the train for the passengers to purchase. There was no food service on the literina, so this was the only source unless you brought some food with you. It was not recommended that we eat this food, as the hygiene of the cooking was not too reliable.

Due to the fact that the stops were often very brief, many of the vendors would board the train and ride with us to the next stop. In this way they had a much better opportunity to sell their wares, and the quality of the crafts was amazing. They had woodcarvings, elaborate hangings made from small patches of llama or alpaca hides that they had sewn together, as well as many articles woven from the wool of these animals. The vendors would bargain for a price, and as we approached the next stop the prices would drop quickly. I was able to purchase several pieces from the vendors and have always cherished them. Upon arrival at the next town, the vendors would disembark and wait for the next train going back to their hometown. Hopefully they made enough profit to pay for the round trip. It was also doubtful that they could return the same day since the train schedule was very limited, just as Steve and Sue had found out—getting to Corumbá a day ahead of me still got them on the same train. Making a living in the interior of Bolivia was not easy in 1971.

Upon our arrival in Santa Cruz, we went to the home of a Mrs. Kline. She had boarded Peace Corps volunteers before the revolution and was very glad to see Steve and Sue again. Over dinner Mrs. Kline filled us in on the details of the revolution, as much of the fighting had taken place in Santa Cruz. She said, "I am so glad that all of you were able to get out of Bolivia before the fighting started. It was the most frightening thing that I have ever experienced in my long life. With all the planes, firing rockets, and the machinegun fire, we were sure that we would not survive. Fortunately the fighting did not last too many days and we made it through. I don't know what the army would have done to you kids if they had found you here. They were rounding up as many students as they could, and you might have been mistaken for one of them." The university students in Santa Cruz had for the most part backed the former government. The air force attacked the university buildings as a result of this alliance, and although they only had five aircraft the air force shot up the buildings pretty badly. Wandering around Santa Cruz the day after our arrival, we observed many bullet holes in storefronts, through display cases, and into the interior walls. Due to the fact that we were about the same age as the students who had backed the former government, we felt quite uncomfortable walking around. There were military guards on every street corner carrying submachine guns.

Bolivian governments after the 1952 revolution were generally committed to capitalism with a state control in the interest of social justice. General Juan Torres, who came from a humble background, ran Bolivia from 1970 until 1971 and was very popular. Colonel Hugo Banzar Suarez deposed him in the revolution of 1971. With the removal of Torres, the Peace Corps volunteers were no longer welcome in Bolivia. Banzar brought more political repression but also economic growth.

We could have stayed longer in Santa Cruz, but Steve and Sue wanted to get on to Cochabamba. The armed-camp atmosphere in the city did not make it terribly inviting to us, either.

9/25/71

We flew from Santa Cruz to Cochabamba since we were told that the bus trip up through the mountains would be suicidal. Buses were lost down the sides of mountains all the time as a result of poorly maintained roads. The idea of tumbling down a slope inside a Bolivian bus was not very appealing to the three of us. I was beginning to get a real appreciation for how good the roads were in the developed world. This even applied to Brasil, where I had often felt that the roads weren't all that great. The flight only cost eleven dollars—not a lot for our lives!

Upon arriving in Cochabamba, we went to the home of Bob and Lyn, two graduate students from Stanford University. They were anthropologists studying the market structures of the Indians living high in the Andes. The natives in those regions only spoke Quechua. Bob and Lyn spoke the language well and knew many of the Indians. By this time I was really glad that I was traveling with Steve and Sue. They spoke Spanish (my Portuguese helped a lot, but it wasn't Spanish) and knew all these interesting people.

Bob and Lyn had a Jeep, so we went way up into the mountains to several Indian markets. We had the opportunity of conversing with the Indians (with Bob and Lyn translating, of course) about their goods. I purchased several items directly from the artisans, which would not have been possible elsewhere. The Indians of the high Andes (especially around La Paz) often have a form of tuberculosis that remains in check if they stay at high altitudes. If the Indians come down for extended periods of time, the tuberculosis flares up and they die. For this reason, the people selling the goods at tourist markets are not the ones who produced the items. It was a real privilege to meet these wonderful Indian artisans.

While we stayed with Bob and Lyn, we passed the time at night learning several Indian games, like "Cacho." It is an interesting dice game which can be played almost anywhere. While waiting for a bus or passing time in the evening, it replaced television or other diversions that were unavailable to the Indians. The game is very popular in all parts of Bolivia and other surrounding countries. It is played with five dice and a cup, making it inexpensive and easy to carry around. I purchased a set and it is still in perfect working order after all these years. Two or more people can play Cacho, but with more than about six it gets a little complicated. Play goes around to the left until each player has ten turns. Each turn consists of up to three rolls of the dice. All the dice are rolled the first time, and then the roller may choose to roll any number of dice on subsequent rolls. The object is to make any of the ten scoring combinations. Each player has a scoring grid, where the results of the rolls are marked down. The combinations are for as many of each of the six numbers as you can roll. The dots are then added up. There is also a straight five, which is worth twenty-five points. A full house is worth thirty points. (This is worth thirty-five points if done in one roll.) Four of a kind is worth forty points. (This is worth forty-five if done in one roll.) Finally, there is the grande, or five of a kind. This is worth fifty points. A grande thrown on one roll wins the game automatically. Obviously this is just a brief idea of how the game is played, and there are many variations of the rules. It would take more space than I have room for here to elaborate further. I highly recommend the game, and I am sure that is available somewhere on the Internet.

9/29/71

We finally left the hospitality of Bob and Lyn and caught a ferro-bus (another type of train-bus) to La Paz, Bolivia. The trip through the mountains was spectacular. The three of us were also happy to be traveling on sturdy steel rails and not over a dirt road, which could collapse and dump us down into a ravine. The terrain in Bolivia is not conducive to road building, and as a result land travel between cities is a little risky. The scenery along the route is something that the typical tourist, flying at altitude, never has the opportunity to witness. The trains travel on a narrow, level area dug into the sides of the mountains. It is nearly vertical both above and below, giving the traveler a great view at all times. After dark, we finally arrived in La Paz. Upon arrival at the city either by train or airplane, travelers enter from around 13,300 feet. La Paz has the highest commercial airport in the world. You then descend to around 12,300 feet, and if you are fortunate enough to arrive at night, as we did, the city looks like a huge bowl filled with candles. We headed to the Hotel Austria, near Plaza Murillo, as it was recommended to Peace Corps volunteers. Many hotels in South America gave discounts at the time and this was one of them. As was also the case with many hotels in South America, there was a business of some type on the ground floor, and the hotel lobby was on the second floor. I carried my big leather bag up the stairs, walked up to the front desk, started to request a room, and promptly passed out!

I awoke to Steve and Sue saying, "Are you all right?"

I replied, "Yes, I'm fine, I guess the altitude was more than I expected." I finally recovered and checked into my room for a good night's sleep. The cost of the room, in 1971, was only $1.25 per night.

9/30/71

In the morning we headed out into the city to do some sightseeing and to get our paperwork done at immigration. Just as was the case leaving Brasil, there was a mass of bureaucracy to cut through in order to leave Bolivia and enter Peru. This bureaucratic work could sometimes take days to accomplish, so we wanted to get it started as soon as possible. As it turned out, we were able to get our visas for Peru quite easily and hoped for the best at the border crossing the next day.

The city, as I mentioned earlier, is laid out in a bowl-shaped valley. The streets are very steep as they go up the sides of the valley. The large Indian population (about half of the residents) lives in the upper parts of the city. If you go uphill, especially on Camacho and Calle Buenos Aires, there are markets where all types of Indian goods can be purchased. During the weekends these markets expand, and almost anything produced in Bolivia can be found there.

The richer part of La Paz is in the bottom part of the bowl, where it is easier to get around. There is also more oxygen here, making the breathing less laborious. As it was our first day at that altitude, we took it easy. One fact that we learned while in La Paz was that until the late sixties the city had never had a fire department. It was felt that there was so little oxygen that fires had little chance of getting out of hand once they got started. In order to modernize the city, fire-fighting equipment was purchased, but it got little use. Even fire has to take it easy that high up! La Paz also lays claim to being the highest capitol city in the world.

Another thing that I should mention is the rapid changes in temperature. Most of the residents of the city wear ponchos, and this is for good reason. Even though the daily temperature is quite pleasant (it rarely goes below freezing), when a cloud covers the sun the temperature can drop over ten degrees. This sudden drop could create a problem if one is not prepared. If one is wearing a poncho, however, one simply rolls it out over one's arms to be quite comfortable. When the sun returns, the poncho is rolled back up, cooling one off.

For the adventurous looking for a real climate change, a four-hour bus ride over the Andes puts travelers in a steaming jungle. We did not have the time for this side trip and I have regretted it for a long time. The difference between the arid western side of the Andes and their lush, jungle-covered eastern slopes is remarkable. It is also quite difficult to get to these areas, so to have missed such an opportunity by only a four-hour bus ride was a real shame. In the southern Andes near Santiago, Chile, the difference in climates is reversed. The western slopes are very lush, with waterfalls and dense vegetation. At higher elevations the water freezes and one encounters frozen waterfalls and famous ski areas, like Portillo. After passing through a two-mile tunnel to the Argentine side of the Andes, one passes through miles and miles of desert until just east of Mendoza. The predominant westerly winds in these lower latitudes push moist sea air up the western slopes of the Andes, but the moisture cannot get over the top. Hence the desert conditions on the eastern side.

We felt we had been in Bolivia long enough, so we purchased tickets for a train-boat-train ride to Cuzco, Peru. First class was twenty dollars, and a second class was only eight! I have always enjoyed going to movies, and since there were several theaters near our hotel, the three of us went to see *The Only House in London.*

10/01/71

We spent most of the day seeing the richer part of the city and then caught the train to Guaqui. Guaqui is the port city for Bolivia on the shore of Lake Titicaca, nearly a thousand feet below the lip of the bowl surrounding La Paz. The trip, all downhill after the bus ride out of the bowl, took the rest of the daylight hours, and we were glad to finally see the amazing expanse of the lake as we approached it from above.

Upon the train's arrival at sunset in Guaqui, we disembarked and were immediately stripped of our passports and herded into a warehouse. Armed guards were posted outside until the steamship we had tickets for arrived. It had been a little uncomfortable in Bolivia, so soon after the revolution, but being held in a warehouse was becoming downright scary! From time to time, agents of some sort came into the warehouse and questioned groups of passengers. My limited grasp of Spanish left me somewhat in the dark, but Steve and Sue said, "This is not looking good. We're not sure if we are going to be allowed to leave the country when the steamer arrives."

It appeared that they wanted to know why any non-Bolivian or Peruvian nationals were traveling on trains and boats. Most foreigners traveled between cities by airplane and did not show up in locations like this. When it was our turn to explain, Steve told me, "Don't try to answer. I'll tell them that you are traveling with us and don't speak Spanish." Steve told the agents that we wanted to see the real Bolivia and not the "four-star hotel" one that regular tourists would see. This explanation seemed to please the agents, and they thanked us for taking an interest in their country. Apparently they were tired of rich tourists coming to see how the "third world" lived. We were finally escorted to the ship and told that we would have our passports returned to us after clearing Peruvian customs.

Upon boarding the ship, I met a Swiss girl named Geneve. She was traveling alone like me. She had seen much of South America and was now heading north to Central America and finally the United States. Geneve was tired of not having anyone to share her experiences with and was very glad for some company. Since she spoke at least four languages, communicating in English was no problem. We were now a couple, and I didn't feel like the odd man out as I had before with Steve and Sue.

The entire trip from La Paz to Cuzco took approximately twenty-eight hours. The portion on Lake Titicaca, which is the highest navigable lake in the world, was about half that time. Our steamship was the *Ollanta*, a 260-foot steel ship built in Hull, England. She was constructed in 1929 and then disassembled and sent to Peru. The parts were then carried up into the Andes by train and reassembled on Lake Titicaca. The ship had accommodations for seventy passengers. The *Ollanta* fell into disrepair sometime after my journey, but fortunately she was taken over by Peru Rail (the Orient Express) and is currently being refurbished to once again carry passengers on lake cruises.

The first steamships to travel on the lake were also built in England. They were the *Yavari* and the *Yapura*, built in 1862. They were shipped to Peru in pieces small enough to be carried up the mountains by mules! There was no railroad to the lake at that time. The parts for the two ships were to be carried up to the lake over a six-month period. Due to many delaying factors such as Indian revolts, earthquakes, and threats of war, the *Yavari* was finally reconstructed and launched in 1870. The *Yapura* was launched in 1873. These first two ships were originally purchased as gunboats, but the Peruvian navy took the guns to defend against the Spanish. The ships were built with steam engines and fueled with llama dung! These engines were replaced in 1914 with semi-diesel engines. The *Yavari* was grounded and left to rust in the 1980s, and luckily a British woman, Meriel Larken, is working to put her back into full service. The ship made her first new voyage in 2006. She is expected to pass certification for carrying passengers on lake cruises in 2008. The *Yapura* was converted to a hospital ship which serves the small towns around the lake. It is amazing that these ships ever got to the lake in the first place, but that they are still steaming about at 12,500 feet above sea level is a miracle.

Chapter 3: Peru

10/02/71

The trip across Lake Titicaca was really spectacular, with blue water all around and the amazing snow-capped Andes Mountains to the east. It was a very romantic setting to say the least. For a couple of twenty-something travelers like Geneve and me, it didn't take long for us to get very well acquainted. We had both been traveling single for some time, and this opportunity gave our adolescent hormones an outlet. The term, "shipboard romance" took on new meaning for me!

We traveled all night on the lake. When the sun finally rose, we could see the mountains to the east again looking like a row of jagged white teeth. The northern end of the lake, which lay in Peru, was also now visible.

The Uru Indians live on the lake. They have villages on islands made of reeds, and rarely set foot on dry land. They get about in boats, also made of reeds, and live on a diet of mainly fish. Their boats are similar in style to those seen in Egypt on the Nile and were the inspiration for Thor Heyerdahl's raft, the *Ra II*. Heyerdahl sailed his raft across the Atlantic in 1970 from Morocco to Barbados. The voyage proved the theory that the people from Africa could have made the trip on a similar craft. The *Ra II* was made of reeds from Lake Titicaca with technical help from the Uru Indians.

Customs in Peru was nothing like the treatment we had received in Bolivia, so we cleared easily. Our passports were returned to us, and we boarded the train for Cuzco, Peru. Cuzco is actually over a thousand feet below the level of Lake Titicaca, so it was a downhill trip to the city. The train traveled through many valleys along the route, and we got a real impression of the verticality of the Andes. This was another perspective that tourists traveling between cities by plane do not get to experience.

The train arrived at night, and the four of us checked into the Hotel Trinitarias on Calle Trinitarias. The cost for a double room was eighty cents a night! This hotel had a great deal if one was going to Machupicchu. A room could be rented for one night, then on the second day and night one could store one's bags for free while visiting the ruins, and then on the third night one could stay in the same room. We took this option, and it was comforting to know that a bed awaited us when we returned, dead tired, from Machupicchu.

10/03/71

We spent the day seeing the city of Cuzco, which is one of the best examples of Inca stonework that can be found in the world. When the Spanish conquered the Inca in the 1500s, they used the stone structures they found and built upon them. Most of the Inca buildings were single story, so the upper stories of today's buildings are Spanish. The difference in building ability is very apparent when you see the division between the first Inca floor and the upper Spanish floors. The Inca stones are cut in all sizes and shapes, with no two the same. The amazing thing is that the seams between the stones are so perfect that a razor blade could not fit between them! There is one huge stone, now part of the Archbishop's Palace, which is referred to as "the stone of twelve angles." It is considered a masterpiece since it has eight outside corners and four inside corners on its outer edge. Other stones, and there are eleven of them, are then fitted into these angles, all with no mortar of any kind.

The city, which had a population of about ninety thousand at the time I visited, was still very much like it was at the time of the Spanish occupation. Probably 99 percent of the residents were of Indian decent and the culture had not changed very much at all. The conquistadores had sought gold and found it by the ton. There is much evidence of this in the churches of Cuzco, where they left a large part of the gold as icons and adornments. The streets of the city were still paved with cobblestones, and the residents still dressed much as they did for the prior four hundred years. Walking the streets of Cuzco was like living in the past except for the few tourists we saw.

In 1533, the Inca capitol of Cuzco was the largest city in the western hemisphere. When Francisco Pizarro found it, there was more gold there than the Spanish had ever dreamed of finding. In one year they ended one of the greatest civilizations that had ever existed and razed the city to its foundations. The Spanish-style buildings, built on top of the Inca foundations, are impressive, but do not have the quality workmanship, that the Incas practiced.

The center of the city is the Plaza de Armas, which is the site of the most impressive Inca walls and temple. The massive Inca temple of the sun is about two blocks from the plaza, and there are more than a dozen churches just in the center of the city. We went inside several of these, but it would have taken many days to see all of them. There are huge gilded altars inside the churches. The Church of Belen, the Compania Church, and the cathedral are especially impressive. Many churches have ornately carved cedar pulpits and choir lofts. An Indian master carver supposedly carved the pulpit in the San Blas Church, and his scull is built into the pulpit under a statue of Saint Thomas!

Within a few miles of the city, there are Incan fortresses used to defend the city from attack. They were built of massive stone blocks, some weighing over five hundred tons. These blocks were transported over a mile and then erected in the same manner as the walls of Cuzco. There have been numerous earthquakes in Peru over the centuries, but these walls have remained intact. Many of the Spanish upper stories in Cuzco have fallen, as was the case in a 1950 quake that damaged much of the Santo Domingo Church. We wanted to see Machupicchu, however, so we did not have time to go see the fortresses.

10/04/71

We took the first-class train early in the morning to Machupicchu. We had purchased the tickets the day before and were told to go first class, as second class was in basically cattle cars with no amenities whatsoever.

The cost at the time for first class was seventy-five cents. The seventy-mile train trip on a narrow-gauge track took about three hours. Since there was no highway, this was the only way to get to our destination. The scenery that we passed, dropping down the Urubamba River, was spectacular. The canyon undulates down, getting deeper and deeper, as the river descends toward the Amazon.

When we arrived at the end of the train trip, we did not wait for the shuttle bus that takes people to the ruins at the top. We had been informed that a llama herder had a small home near the top with guest rooms available to the first arrivals from the train. It is a fifteen hundred-foot climb up to the ruins by way of the road. The climb is so steep that the road requires thirteen hairpin turns to reach the top. The road was cut out of the rock wall in 1948, and the only way to the ruins before that time was a series of steps cut by the Inca and found by Hiram Bingham in 1911. Of course, the local Indians had always known where it was, but no Anglos had ever seen the ruins until then. After much huffing and puffing, we reached the top before the shuttle bus and got the two rooms available. We paid the royal price of seventy-five cents to stay overnight at what is now one of the modern Seven Wonders of the World! It cost one dollar to see the ruins.

The city of Machupicchu defies description due to its size and layout over the top of the mountain. It was a totally self-sufficient city in that it could produce all that was needed to sustain its population. The purpose of the city was to be both a retreat for the king and a hiding place if he was threatened. Due to the latter use, the city was built in such a way that it cannot be seen from the valley below. All the terraces used to grow food are set back just enough to be hidden from view. The buildings are set back from the terraces and are also not visible. Being at an altitude of eight thousand feet above sea level and in the most inaccessible part of the river valley, the city was never found by the enemies of the Inca. The city is nearly intact except for the timber and grass roofs of the buildings. These would have been repaired or replaced as needed, and they deteriorated once the city was abandoned.

The masonry in the city is much like the walls found in Cuzco. The stone blocks are perfectly cut in random sizes and laid on each other with no mortar. Where possible, niches in the solid rock were filled and spaces created. The uses for the various rooms have been debated, but some of their uses surely remain a mystery. There is evidence that many of the structures were two stories tall, but they still had to stay low enough to not be seen from below. Many other niches were left in the stones on purpose to hold gold ornaments or idols. More than a thousand stairways can be found, allowing the residents to get between the many levels of the city. There are remains indicating where mills and foundries were located, enabling the city to be self-sufficient. Life in Machupicchu was relatively simple and each of the granite houses usually only had one room with a dirt floor. There was little furniture, and the residents would have slept on llama or alpaca skins. Again, niches in the walls were used for storing things instead of cabinets.

We spent the day exploring the city but were unable to climb Huaynapicchu (young peak), as there had been a fire there and it was put off limits to tourists. It was a shame since the view from that peak would have been amazing. When night came, the other day-trippers left and we were alone in the ruins with the llama herder and his llamas. The llamas were allowed to roam free throughout the city, and in this way the grass was kept short and manicured.

Machupicchu was an incredible place to see in the sunlight, but it became truly magical at night. With only the moon to light it and the stars as bright as could be at that altitude, the ruins became a romantic place. The clouds passed through the mountains on a height level with the ruins and were surreal as they went through buildings and around us. It was as if the ghosts of the Incas had come back to inhabit their city for a few hours. Having the llamas wander around added to the magic as well.

If one is lucky enough to be twenty-four and has the great fortune to share a llama herder's guesthouse with a beautiful Swiss girl in a situation like that, it can make for an unforgettable experience! Needless to say, Geneve and I got very little sleep that night, but the memory has lasted.

10/05/71

During the night, Geneve and I had a lot of time to talk about our plans for the days ahead. She said, "I am really enjoying being with you and not traveling alone."

I replied, "I am enjoying this situation as much as you are, but I have transportation paid for all the way to Barbados. It would be nearly impossible for me to cash that in now and change my route."

She looked disappointed and answered, "I really want to see Central America and then travel in the United States."

I was on a trip home and enjoying the adventure, but in reality I had been on a two-year adventure and wanted to get back to the United States before Christmas. We finally came down to the conclusion that our travel plans were not going to fit and we should stick with our original itineraries.

Geneve held me close and whispered, "Maybe this was not our time. Maybe we will meet again if I get to the United States, and then we can rekindle what we had going here."

I told her, "I would like that very much because I feel like there is something happening between us that I would very much like to pursue."

We had to get up early to catch the 8:30 AM train, and we arrived back in Cuzco around 1 PM. I arranged for a ticket to Lima, Peru. This was the first leg of the airline ticket I had purchased in Rio for $230. The ticket would take me to Lima, Guayaquil, Quito, Bogotá, Caracas, Trinidad, and Barbados. The plane ticket from Rio to Philadelphia given to me by the Peace Corps had been worth $380. I could have flown directly home in a few hours, but I now had $150 in travel expense money and was planning on three months of travel time.

I spent some time saying my farewells to Steve and Sue. They had been a great couple to travel with. Their insight into the culture of Bolivia, not to mention their friends that we stayed with, added a great deal to my experience. My trip, up to this point, would have been significantly different had it not been for these two great companions. This was another life lesson for me. Travel is extremely gratifying in itself, but it is twice as rewarding if you can share the experience with someone else. I lost touch with Steve and Sue after I flew to Lima, and do not know what the future held for them.

Finally, I said good-bye to Geneve, who had added that special something that makes a great adventure extra rewarding. Months after returning to the United States, I received a postcard from Geneve. She let me know that she had made it to Costa Rica in Central America and was still heading to the United States. I never heard anything further from her and always hoped she fulfilled her dream of the big adventure. Not everyone would have the courage to travel as she was doing, alone and as a single girl.

10/06/71

I flew to Lima, Peru, and met Peruvian Peace Corps volunteers Bob, Al, Steve, Dave, and Walter. They gave me a tour of the city, and I got to see the National Museum of Anthropology and Archaeology. There is also a fine National Museum of Art. The Plaza de Armas is also quite spectacular, as it is the part of the city that Pizarro first built in 1535. His remains are in a glass coffin in the massive Cathedral. He may have conquered the Incas, but they have his body!

10/07/71

On this dreary day I hired a cab to take me to Punta Hermosa. A few years before this beach town had been the venue for the world surfing championship. I took a cab because the area was not popular enough to warrant bus service. My driver didn't quite understand why anyone would want to go there, but a fare was a fare and off we went. The area was very foggy when I arrived, and the surf would not have challenged even me. Due to the Humboldt Current, which runs along the Peruvian coast, a fog known as the "Garua" is created during the winter months. The fog was present when I was there even though October is actually the start of spring in Peru. The water off the coast of Peru is very cold, so I didn't even do any body surfing. I also didn't see any place to change out of wet clothes if I had gone in the surf. Surfers spend a lot more time looking for waves than they ever do actually surfing. I saw what I had come to see, so I directed my confused driver to take me back to the city.

I wandered around Lima for the rest of the day and was fortunate enough to see President Velasco of Peru. The President was passing by in a motorcade on his way to some important function. The motorcade was moving very slowly so that he could wave to the crowd. General Velasco ruled Peru from 1968 until 1975. He was born in northern Peru, where he graduated from a military school at the top of his class. He rose to the position of Commander of the Armed Forces under then-President Belaunde. During a 1968 oil dispute, Velasco led a military coop, which deposed and exiled President Belaunde. During Velasco's rule, most of Peru's industries were nationalized and leftist policies were introduced. In 1973 the Peace Corps was thrown out, just as had been the case in Bolivia in 1971. By 1975 Velasco's policies had pretty much failed, and there was another military coup. He was deposed and died of an ongoing illness in 1977. The powerful dictator standing erect in his limousine I saw in 1971 only had four more years of rule and a brief time left to live.

Chapter 4: Ecuador

10/08/71

After a late flight, I arrived in Guayaquil, Ecuador, around six in the evening. I was told that there was a celebration for the 151st anniversary of Ecuador. As a result, all the hotels in Guayaquil were full. I eventually found a place called Pension Puerto de Guayas, where patrons are rented space in what was once a warehouse, I think. The owners had divided up the building with plywood partitions and doors. Each boarder was given a lock after paying for that day. The cost was eighty cents per day. I placed the lock on the outside of my space during the day to protect my belongings. Upon returning at night, I placed the lock on the inside of the door to lock others out while I slept. The pension was very near the docks, and the sounds from the other tenants made it quite difficult to sleep soundly. I was glad that Geneve was not with me and forced to occupy accommodations like this. This was certainly not nearly as romantic as the rustic llama herder's rooms had been.

I was able to see the 151st anniversary parade and then had time to wander around much of the city. Since my room was no place that I wanted to rush back to, I went to a movie house and saw *Ryan's Daughter*. One nice feature in 1971 was that movies were shown in English with

Spanish sub-titles. This made it like going to a movie at home with a Spanish lesson added on.

I should mention here that with the anniversary celebration there were more than the normal numbers of street vendors selling every kind of food imaginable. I was able to wander any part of the city with the other celebrants and eat from the vendors' carts whenever I was hungry. Having spent two years living in South America, my digestive system was quite acclimated to almost anything that I put into it. The food was being cooked and eaten as fast as the vendors could get it out to the hungry crowds, so I was pretty secure in not getting anything tainted. Most of the time during my journey, I tried to eat in some kind of restaurant (cheap ones, of course), but in Guayaquil I really enjoyed a huge variety of local fare. One of my favorite things about traveling is trying different kinds of food prepared in the local manner. I always wonder why people would go to France and eat at Burger King.

10/10/71

I was feeling like a duck out of water since I had not been swimming for a month. In Brasil I lived and worked at the beach and went swimming nearly every day. On this day, a group of eleven Peace Corps volunteers invited me to go to a local beach. After about a one-and-a-half-hour bus ride, we arrived at a very nice beach. The long ride only cost forty cents. I was surprised to find that the water temperature was quite warm and not at all like Peru or Chile. We spent the day swimming, and I finally got my water fix. It was also nice to have some company again. I was definitely not alone in Guayaquil, but none of the thousands of people there were with me.

10/11/71

I guess there was something in the water I'd swum in the day before because I woke up with no hearing in my right ear. I spent much of the day trying to solve my problem but to no avail. I finally did what I had done in Brasil—I went to a local pharmacy like the residents would do and got some kind of drops which would probably be illegal in the

United States. The drops helped some, so I spent time seeing more of Guayaquil and tried again to get a boat to the Galapagos Islands.

In 1971, about the only affordable means of transportation to get out to the islands was by way of a slow diesel boat. As luck would have it, the boat was not in working order during the week that I was there. Each day I was told to come back the next day, but the boat was never ready to sail. The alternative method of getting to the Galapagos was as a rich tourist. A round-trip air ticket cost about one hundred dollars. Upon arrival at the islands, you boarded a sixty-passenger cruise yacht called the *Lina-a*. She had been built in 1967. They offered four-day, five-day, and eight-day cruises. The cost per person, in 1971, was $265, $355, and $570, respectively, for the main deck passage. Upper decks were more expensive. All meals on board and ashore were complimentary, as were sightseeing and other costs. This sounds ridiculously cheap today, but compared to my $230 plane ticket from Cuzco to Barbados, it was way out of my reach at the time. I felt that this was a chance of a lifetime to get to the Galapagos Islands and was really disappointed that I couldn't make the trip.

10/12/71

Finally convinced that I was not going to get to the Galapagos Islands, I took a taxi to the airport. I felt that the fare of $1.60 was a rip off. In today's world that fare would be insanely cheap. Remember, I had just been paying eighty cents a night for my room, so this cab cost me the equivalent of two night's sleep!

We had a wonderful flight over the Andes to Quito. The mountains rise up abruptly from the sea to nearly twenty thousand feet and are really impressive as you fly over them en route to Quito. My original plan was to travel this leg of the trip by bus. I took the easy way and included this plane flight in the ticket I bought in Rio. Quito sits almost on the equator and at over nine thousand feet above sea level. It was not as high as La Paz or Cuzco but high enough to slow me down a little.

I checked into the Hotel Europa for the sum of $1.60 a night. The hotel was near the Plaza Independencia, in the heart of the older portion of the city. I took a basic room with no bath. A five-course lunch or dinner could be purchased for $0.80. I preferred to stay in the old city as opposed to the new city. The newer portion was closer to the airport and had more modern buildings and huge mansions. I wanted the feel of the past, not to mention the lower prices. Quito is the second highest capitol in the world and lies in a valley surrounded by the Andes Mountains. Since Quito is almost on the equator, the weather is consistent all year and is similar to New England in the spring. I broke the bank that night and saw two movies, *Horsemen* and *Step in the Dark*, all for $0.24!

10/13/71

In order to finally solve the problem with my right ear, I went to the Peace Corps office in Quito and let the nurse look at it. She said, "You have a bad infection. I think that those drops you bought in Guayaquil should do the trick and cure it in time."

I told her, "Thank God for local pharmacies," and left the office.

Feeling much better about the chances of not losing my hearing, I took Equatoriana de Tourismo's trip to the equator. For the $0.12 price, I was taken to the monument where I could stand with one foot in the northern hemisphere and one foot in the southern hemisphere. On ships at sea and on some airplanes, there is a big celebration when one crosses the equator. At the monument I could cross it as often as I liked by shifting from one foot to the other.

10/14/71

In the morning, I climbed Panacillo, a hill rising six hundred feet above the city. From the vantage point of the top, one can get a great view of this really pretty place. Looking to the north, I could see the dormant volcano Pichincha. This hilltop is the location where General Sucre defeated the Spanish in 1822 to win Ecuador's independence. The city cathedral can also be seen from Panacillo, and it is the burial site of General Sucre. Later that afternoon I took an Avianca Airlines flight to Bogotá, Columbia.

Chapter 5: Columbia

10/14/71

After arriving in Bogotá, I checked into the Hotel Tundama for $3 per night, the Peace Corps rate. The regular rate was $7.25 at that time. This hotel was superior to the new part of the Florida Hotel in Rio, and when in Rio we stayed in the two hundred-year-old portion of the Florida for about $3 per night.

10/15/71

The city of Bogotá lies at 8,600 feet above sea level. Although not as high as La Paz, the thin atmosphere there once again needed to be respected. I went to the famous gold museum, where over ten thousand pieces of pre-Columbian gold are displayed. When touring the museum, small groups are taken by armed guards into a dark room. After the doors are closed, the lights are brought up slowly until tourists realize they are surrounded by more gold than most people will see in a lifetime. It was an impressive sight even to someone like me who doesn't get much out of jewelry. There was an amazing collection of gold pieces from different time periods, but after seeing so much yellow I had had enough. I next went to the National Museum, which was a prison in its past lifetime. This museum contained many artifacts and gave me a glimpse into the history of Columbia. The weather was great on this day, so I took the opportunity to ride the cable car to the top of Monserrate. This breathtaking ride got me to the higher of the two peaks surrounding Bogotá. The ride up is about a 75 percent incline and not for the faint of heart. There is also a funicular railroad, which could be even more frightening. From the mountain-top viewpoint, one gets a bird's-eye view of the city, which is spectacular.

Bogotá, at the time of my trip, was a city of approximately two million residents. There was a mixture of old colonial and modern buildings. In the center of the city is the Plaza Bolivar, and spreading out from the plaza are colonial buildings and mansions. It was a lovely city, even if it did not have a coast nearby. The weather there was a lot damper than in Quito due to the city being surrounded by high mountain peaks. The average daily temperature was around sixty degrees.

10/16/71

On this day, I went underground and toured the largest salt mine in the world, which is near the town of Zipaquira. The mine operators claim that there is enough rock salt to supply the world's needs for one hundred years even though the mine has been in operation for centuries. A cathedral has been carved inside the mine, a feat which required ten years of labor. The roof of the cathedral is seventy-five feet above the floor of the mine, and its altar is a single block of salt weighing eighteen tons. The cathedral measures one hundred by eighty yards and is also carved entirely of rock salt. They like to do things big in Columbia, and this mine certainly was in that tradition. Upon returning to Bogotá, I spent the rest of the day observing the fine architecture that the city has to offer.

10/17/71

My fantastic luck ran out on this day, and it was raining. I had had a great streak of unusual sunny weather, as it is often overcast with frequent rain. Because of the change in weather, I left the city early and went to the airport. The plane was of course delayed for four hours due to this weather. We finally took off at 9:30 PM and arrived in Caracas, Venezuela, just after midnight.

Chapter 6: Venezuela

10/18/71

I slept in the airport and met a couple from Barbados. They graciously said, "Why don't you get in touch with us when you arrive in Barbados. We have a place right on the beach, and we can do some waterskiing and snorkeling."

This sounded too good to be true, so I replied, "You can count on me to take you up on your offer, for sure."

I decided to save some money, so I checked my large duffle bag in a locker at the airport near Caracas. I took one cable car up over the mountains and then another down into the city. The airport for Caracas is located at sea level on the coast. Mount Avila, a nine thousand-foot mountain, is between the airport and the city, which is at three thousand feet. To get to the city, one can take the cheap way as I did or pay for an expensive cab ride all the way around Mount Avila. My large bag would have been a burden in the cable cars, and that is why I left it at the airport. Since I had no real baggage, I got a cheap room and went in search of the Peace Corps office. My cousin was supposed to be a volunteer in Venezuela, but no one at the office knew of her. I met some other volunteers however and was invited for dinner and some good conversation.

10/19/71

I walked around Caracas quite a bit, but it is laid out in a way making it difficult to get around. The city lies in a nine-mile valley. The streets were numbered, but addresses were often given by way of the nearest corner. The practice made it difficult to ask for directions or find a place when directions were given. I had no money for expensive taxicabs or guided tours, so I again took the cable car to the top of the mountain and got fantastic views of both the city and the Caribbean Sea. The sight of the beautiful blue of the Caribbean was calling to me, and I was itching to get to the islands I had longed to see. When I had looked as long as I wanted, I descended to the airport again and spent the night there. Sleeping in airports, back in 1971, was different than it is today. They had nice, comfortable benches and a coffee shop that was open all night. No one hassled me and I got a pretty good night's sleep. With today's crazy airport restrictions, it would probably be impossible to do what I did in Caracas.

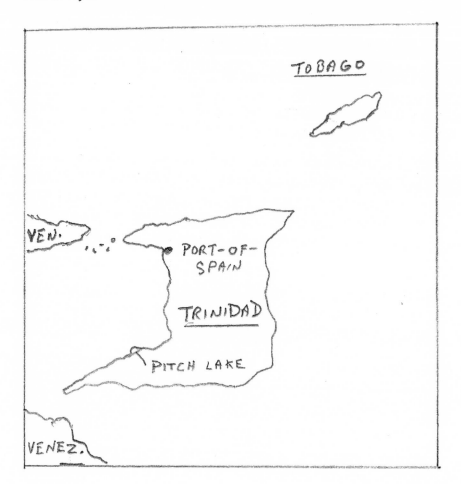

Chapter 7: Trinidad

10/20/71

The next morning, I retrieved my duffle bag from the convenient lockers available at the airport and caught a flight to Trinidad. At last, after two years, I was in a country where English was the official spoken language. In the airport, all the announcements were spoken in perfect British English, and I was feeling great until I reached the taxi stand outside. At this point the language morphed into something I had never heard before and could not understand. I eventually got my driver to take me to the home of a Miss Bryan. She had rented rooms to Peace Corps volunteers in my brother's training group in 1969. Miss Bryan was a schoolteacher and lived just outside Port of Spain, the capitol of Trinidad and Tobago. Being a teacher, she spoke perfect "Queen's English," and we had a good time reminiscing about the volunteers who had stayed with her. She said, "I'll have one of my friends take you on a tour of the city." When her friend arrived, they both started speaking in the local tongue. They had great fun messing with my head, but finally the friend gave me a break and spoke English so that I could understand. The patois spoken by the citizens of Trinidad and Tobago comes from the various countries that exerted control over the islands during their history.

Columbus discovered the islands in 1498, and Arawak and Carib Indians had occupied both of the islands before his arrival. I always loved the idea that these islands were not discovered until 1498 or whenever. I wonder if the Arawak and Caribs felt lost until then. Both of these tribes were very territorial groups and did not welcome Europeans to their shores. Since the Spanish found no gold on either island, they left them alone. When agriculture proved to be possible in the 1700s, Spain took control of Trinidad, and England took Tobago. By 1803, the British had control of both islands, and their control led to the current use of English as the official language.

Miss Bryan's friend and I had a nice tour of Port of Spain. The city is home to most of the roughly one million citizens of Trinidad. Most of the land area is mountainous or agricultural, leaving little room for housing. The city is also the major port where the crops, grown in the country, are shipped out along with the petroleum products that make up most of the country's exports. In the southwest is Pitch Lake, from where asphalt is taken, as well as oil from wells. Today, tourism has become a large factor in the economy, and windsurfing and scuba diving bring many foreigners to the islands. None of that was in existence in 1971, so there was little for me to see or do on Trinidad or Tobago. After a good traditional island dinner and a night's sleep, I bid Miss Bryan and Trinidad farewell and flew to Barbados.

Chapter 8: Barbados

This was the last leg of the airline ticket that I had purchased in Rio back in September. From this point on, I was going to have to plan my trip as I went. After clearing customs in the Barbados airport (yes, that song and dance again), I got a taxi to Bridgetown and found the Peace Corps office. I was looking for Lee Franklin, a volunteer who had trained with my brother in 1969. Luckily for me, Lee was at the office when I arrived.

On Barbados, things were different for the Peace Corps than I had been used to in Brasil. The volunteers there had nice new motorcycles and rented much nicer houses than we had been able to. When Lee was finished with his work for the day, we got on his bike and rode to his two-bedroom house. He had graciously invited me to stay for a while if I would chip in for food, help him cook, and generally assist with the daily chores. My plan was to stay a few days, see the island, find a boat to the main island chain (Barbados is one hundred miles east of the Windward Island chain), and then find a job on a charter boat heading north. As you will see, the plan changed somewhat, and my stay on Barbados was a bit longer.

10/22/71

On my first full day in Barbados, I got a chance to wander around Bridgetown, the capitol of the country. It is the island's main harbor and also the hub of the excellent bus system that can take people almost anywhere on the island. The only drawback to the system was that almost all buses started and finished their routes in Bridgetown, so if one wished to go from one town to another that was not on the same route, one had to take a bus to Bridgetown and then a second bus to one's destination. This system resulted in a lot of time traveling on multiple buses to get between two relatively close towns. But the system worked and it beat walking. The island is only twenty-one miles long by fifteen wide, so it's never too far to anywhere, anyway.

I spent some time shopping for an 8mm movie camera to replace the one I had taken to Brasil. When I was a senior in college I attended a movie festival at the end of the year. Film students were able to show the films they had made during the semester. At the end of the festival, a drawing was held using the ticket stubs, and prizes were awarded. To my amazement, I held the winning ticket for the grand prize! I won an 8mm camera, and I learned to use that basic camera around school. When I went to Brasil, I took it along to document my experience. Unfortunately, the expense of developing film in Brasil was too high for a Peace Corps salary, so I sent the exposed film back to the United States to be processed. The time delay between sending letters home and receiving a response was sometimes three weeks to a month. I had to wait for the film to be developed and then wait for a letter telling me of the results. Occasionally, the folks back home would wait until they had several rolls before sending them off to be developed. The net result of all this was that many of the rolls of film turned out to be all black when developed, and I was unaware of it. I presume that the film was subjected to X-ray machines in customs and was ruined. I have less than one hour of usable film from two years and countless rolls exposed. The original camera started to develop a halo of mold growing inside the lens due to the high humidity in Brasil. We had no air conditioning in those days. I sold the camera before leaving for home and planned to purchase a new and more sophisticated one when I got to a duty-free port. Barbados was full of duty-free shops, and there was a good selection of cameras. I just had to make up my mind as to what features I wanted and how much I could afford on my tight budget.

That night I got a wild ride on the back of Lee's motorcycle when we went to the United States Navy PX. The PX was on Barbados to serve the Navy personnel stationed there at the time. Since Peace Corps volunteers were government employees, they were able to purchase anything they wanted at the PX. The prices were lower than anywhere in the United States at the time. This PX had virtually anything you could want. There were televisions, stereos, the latest albums, clothing, everything. This was not the Peace Corps I had just been in!

I had lived in a little house with no glass in the windows. We had marginal electricity that caused the lights to flicker and the clocks to run fast and then slow, but never on time. Our water came from the roof cistern and the toilet only flushed when we poured water into it from a bucket. We were given an allowance to buy a bicycle when we arrived, so we could go anywhere we wanted as long as we kept pedaling. I am glad that I didn't know of the differences between levels of living conditions earlier. By living under the conditions that we did in Brasil, we fit into the culture there much better than we would have if we had lived like the government personnel in Rio, for example. I would not give up those two years in Brasil for anything.

10/23/71

The next day, full of fond memories of my pedaling days in Brasil, I went to the Peace Corps office and borrowed a bicycle. I could now get around the island easier if I didn't try to go too far. To my amazement, I was told that to ride a bike you were required to have a license! I obtained my documents and headed to Bridgetown to purchase my new camera. I was able to buy a Vivitar super 8, with a zoom lens, filters, and a nice case for only one hundred dollars. With my new prize possession, I headed out to film the beaches of Barbados. I started with Silver Sands and South Shore, which were not too long a bike ride from Lee's house. These surfing spots were virtually unknown in 1971, but that would not last forever. They were too good to stay hidden from the world of surfers, who are always looking for the perfect wave.

10/24/71

I decided to pay a visit to the couple I had met in the Caracas airport, Ron and Joan. Ron was an architect with a work visa, and they were staying in a lovely beach house in the Payne's Bay area. The bay is on the quiet west side of Barbados. Ron and I went snorkeling, my first time since leaving Brasil. I had been carrying my mask and fins for the whole trip so that I would have them when I arrived in the Caribbean. The clarity of the waters around Barbados was the best that I had ever witnessed. Ron and Joan called for a water-ski boat, and I was able to enjoy a sport that I had not been able to participate in for a long time. My arms really suffered the next day, but this day at the beach gave me an insight into how one could live if one was self-employed and could earn a decent amount of money. I, of course, had no idea what I would be doing with my education when I returned to the United States, but it is always nice to dream big.

10/25/71

Having mastered the bus system by this time, I ventured out to the east coast of Barbados. I stopped for a bit in Martin's Bay, where there were some nice waves, and then moved on to Bathsheba. I grew up in New Jersey, where a three to five-foot wave is pretty good size. At Bathsheba, the wave faces were at least ten to twelve feet on a regular day! The bay is U-shaped and about a mile across. It is very steep and sandy in the middle, but it has sheer coral rock cliffs on either side. Due to the shape of the beach, there is a strong current that runs out the center toward the open sea. While I was there, filming the waves and the surfers riding them, I met a group of the surfers. The guys were from New Jersey, New York, Florida, and California. They were renting a small cottage on the hill overlooking the bay. To save money they were living on bread and cheese, washed down with local beer and rum. This was another lifestyle that required no formal education or a great deal of money. The famous film by Bruce Brown, *The Endless Summer*, did not feature Barbados. One could live the lifestyle from that movie here without traveling at all. It is always summer in Barbados, and the waves of Bathsheba, and those of her other beaches, are nearly perfect.

10/26/71

Since I had such a good time the day before, I took the bus back to Bathsheba again the next day. I shot more movies of the guys surfing and was offered a surfboard to try my luck. By 1971, the sport of surfing had evolved some, and the boards that these very proficient surfers were using were only about five to six feet long. I had done most of my surfing on the smaller waves of New Jersey with a nine-and-a-half-foot Greg Noll "Cat." The difference, to a non-surfer, is like day and night. Since I was twenty-four and stupid, I took up the offer and paddled out. I managed to catch a few waves and get back out without killing myself. Instead of quitting while I was ahead, I went out for another wave and lost the board near the beach. I was in waist-deep water, but since the beach was so steep, I couldn't get out. The returning water from the previous wave was so strong that it pushed me back out to sea. When I turned around, I noticed the next ten-foot wall of water ready to break on me! A ten-foot wave can crush you, so I did the only proper thing and dove under it. Body surfing these waves would have been suicidal, so I was now stuck outside the break.

I swam toward the beach for about half an hour, and due to the current I was about a quarter mile out to sea. Swimming to either side of the beach was not an option since the sand ended against fifty-foot high cliffs, where the waves just pounded. Luckily for me, the guy who had loaned me his board noticed that it was up on the beach and that I was not with it. He finally spotted me and paddled out to my rescue. We both surfed in on the board lying down. No one used leashes on their boards like they do today, for that would have prevented this whole episode in the first place. I found out that if you didn't ride your board all the way up the steep beach until it ground to a stop, you were in big trouble.

On the brighter side, while I was recovering from my ordeal I met a Canadian girl named Jill Banks who was there on vacation. Jill had hired a taxi to take her all the way to the east coast of the island and was not sure how she would get back. I told her all about the island bus system and volunteered to guide her back to her hotel.

We had a nice dinner at the Holiday Inn, where she was staying, and took a long walk on the beach later. The beaches on Barbados are all public property, so you can walk in front of any hotels or houses if there is some sand. After the romantic, moonlit walk, we decided to go for a swim out to a floating platform by the Holiday Inn. Well, one thing led to another, and let me just say that my chivalry that afternoon led to some very just rewards! I was sure glad that I had not expired that afternoon and vowed to be more careful when surfing in the future. Jill had plans for the next day, so we agreed to meet on the twenty-eighth, for some sightseeing.

10/27/71

In my travels around the island looking for surfing spots to film, I met several local surfers. They were very leery at first to talk about their favorite breaks or to have me film them. All surfers are territorial and do not like additional people showing up at their favorite beaches. These guys were very proud of the excellent surf around Barbados, and they didn't want to share their waves with the horde of tourists that might show up if the word got out about how great the surfing was. The group that I had met in Bathsheba was an example of how knowledge of a good spot could bring in more surfers. The Bruce Brown film *The Endless Summer* had sparked a worldwide search for untried surfing venues. The locals in Barbados didn't want their island to be the next hot spot.

I finally convinced some of the locals I had met that I wasn't filming to promote their waves—it was only for my memories. They took pity on me, traveling on my bicycle, and invited me to travel around the island in search of the perfect wave. Ian (owner of a mini-truck), Mike, Pat, and Rich would pick me up in the morning at Lee's house, and we would spend the day driving around the perimeter of Barbados searching for waves. Being locals, they had a pretty good idea of which beaches would have the best waves, under the conditions, on any given day. We would usually find excellent places to surf. On this day, we went to Rockley Beach and caught some nice waves. This beach, which by the time of this book's publication has become a well-known windsurfing location (yes, the word did finally get out), is a good place at high tide. When the tide goes out, you must deal with thousands of black spiny sea urchins that carpet the bottom near the shore. During high tide, if you lose your board you can swim to retrieve it. When the tide is out, however, there isn't enough water to pass over the urchins, and getting to the beach is a painful experience!

Later in the day, I went to the post office to see if I had any mail. I also wanted to mail my old 35mm camera back to a friend in Brasil. My best Brasilian friend had always wanted a camera, but they were too expensive in Brasil. I had told him that I would send him my camera when I purchased a replacement. Once again my good intensions failed. The camera was at my parent's house when I returned to the United States. It had gone to Brasil but couldn't be delivered, and it was forwarded to the return address, my parent's house.

10/28/71

On this sunny day, I met with Jill again and we took a bus trip to Speitstown, which is on the quiet west coast of Barbados. The beach north of town was fairly isolated, and the water was perfectly clear and great for snorkeling. When we arrived, Jill let me know that she had not gotten the idea that we were going to go swimming on the trip and had not brought a suit. As I mentioned earlier, Jill was on vacation from work. What I did not reveal was that she owned a massage parlor in Canada.

She said, "It doesn't bother me that I don't have a bikini with me. I'll just go like this." Upon saying those words, she stripped off her sundress and panties and hit the water! After a brief swim in the sea, she returned to the beach, where I had stripped to my bathing suit. The sight of Jill coming out of the water holds for me a memory much like that of Halle Berry coming out of the sea to greet James Bond in *Die Another Day*. The big difference for me is that imagining the body without a bathing suit wasn't necessary! Jill's return from the water was, to say the least, quite arousing.

She said, "Let's not waste this opportunity. I know just what to do with that." She spent the following hour demonstrating the skills she was taking a vacation from. I can truthfully say that her patrons in Canada must be some very happy customers. This turned out to be a sort of busman's holiday, and I was very pleased to be the passenger on the bus!

As I mentioned, this was a fairly deserted stretch of beach, but I did hear tires squeal a number of times as passing motorists hit the brakes to get a better look at the naked Canadian on the sand. It was a wonderful day, but it was finally over. And like all good things, so was my time with Jill. She had to fly back to Canada the next day and left me with only memories. I guess that is why many singles go to sunny Caribbean islands—to make memories with people they will never see again.

10/29/71

Back to my old routine, I met up with Ian again and we went to Brandon's Beach and caught some seven-foot waves. My ability level was improving, and with the lack of steepness at Bathsheba, I was able to ride these larger waves.

That night, we went to a party (it's great to know the natives) and really enjoyed ourselves. Ian and the other guys got a little too drunk to drive, so I was made the designated driver. If you have never been to Barbados, they drive on the left as in England. I had never driven on the left side before. With way too much rum in me to be operating a vehicle, this was quite a trip. Away from the main towns, the roads on Barbados are extremely narrow and winding. They also pass through miles and miles of sugar cane (where the rum comes from), which stands about eight feet high when mature. I had no idea where I was or how to get back to Ian's house. Driving these winding roads, with headlights appearing suddenly on the wrong side of the road, was frightening to say the least. Somehow, and I have no memory of it, we all got back to where we belonged and no harm came to any of us. I guess the night was a final bonding, since Ian and Gregg, another surfer from Ian's tribe, decided to accompany me when I finally found a ride to the main island chain.

10/30/71

I went down to the docks again in Bridgetown and searched for a boat going west to the main island chain. In 1971, inter-island commerce was still carried out by small freighters. Some of these were diesel powered, and some still used sails. I was hoping to hitch a ride on a charter sailboat, but they mainly stayed along the main chain of Caribbean islands and did not venture the one hundred miles east to Barbados. In truth my choices were limited to commercial vessels carrying goods between the islands. I had no luck that day, so I went to the hippodrome, or horse track, and saw some local action. The British are really into horse racing, and Barbados is still a little slice of Britain in many ways.

10/31/71

On this day, I paid back some of the kindness that I had received from the Peace Corps volunteers on Barbados. We all helped Butch, another volunteer, move to a new job location on Martin's Bay. Butch was helping to set up cooperative grocery stores, which was very similar to my work with fishing cooperatives in Brasil. I have reminisced a lot about my surfing and sightseeing, but I also spent a lot of time with Lee and the other volunteers doing basic day-to-day things. The volunteers had work to do all day while I was surfing and exploring the island. At night we would get together and listen to music or just do what twenty-year-olds do. I was glad to be back in the company of people my age from the same cultural background. In Brasil I rarely spent much time with Americans, except for the time that I spent with Marc and Linda the first year.

11/01/71

I went back to Bridgetown again and finally got lucky. A small island freighter was going to Bequia (pronounced beck-way), which is just south of Saint Vincent. The owner of the boat lived on Bequia and was going home after delivering his cargo in Saint Vincent. He said that the trip would take overnight and that we were welcome to sleep on deck for the voyage. Ian and Gregg planned to go over with me and then come back in about a week when the boat returned to Barbados. That night we celebrated by going to a touristy nightspot called the Island Club. At the club, I met a charter boat captain from Washington State who claimed to make thirty-five thousand dollars a year. Here was another idea for what to do for a living; all I needed was a beautiful charter boat.

11/02/71

I went to Payne's Bay again and did some snorkeling. Since I had seen so many fish on my first visit, I figured that the location warranted a return visit. I had been carrying my mask and fins from Brasil through my whole trip since I knew this would be a chance of a lifetime to snorkel. Growing up in New Jersey had given me a chance to learn snorkeling, but the visibility and assortment of fish to view there can't compare to the Caribbean. The snorkeling in Brasil had been better than New Jersey, but the clarity of the ocean there varied dramatically with the seasons and the amount of rainfall. That night I went freshwater crayfish hunting with Lee and Sealy another Peace Corps volunteer. We were quite successful and cooked our catch. It provided a meal that may be only topped by fresh Maine Lobster.

11/03/71

I had the opportunity to drive around the island for the last time with Ian and saw most of the beaches. There was Duppie's, with enormous waves, on the northwest coast. Duppie's is also famous for its large sharks, so surfing there is a gamble. If one climbs way down to the water from the road above, one can paddle out and catch waves that last for at least a quarter of a mile. We also went to Bat Rock and Animal Flower Cave. The cave is open to the sea on the east coast and is accessible from above by way of a ladder. When the surf is really high, it can enter the cave to some extent. People have been swept out of the cave on occasion. The cave gets its name from the beautiful anemones that live in the pools of water on the cave's floor. If one approaches the pools very carefully, the "flowers" stay open for a moment before pulling back into their holes quickly. Anemones like these live on most tropical reefs, but they are rarely visible to admirers from above the water.

Toward the end of the day, we met three stewardesses on vacation between flights. Cindy, Jinny, and Janice drove around the east coast with us that night and fulfilled our expectations of what a date with a stewardess would be like.

11/04/71

I went back to Bat Rock and Sandy Lane and did some final surfing and snorkeling. In Barbados, the conditions for these activities are world-class. Who knew when I would get to return to Barbados again? As it turns out, I've been back three times since, but I didn't know that in 1971. I have learned from other missed opportunities that one should do things when possible. If the chance comes again that's wonderful, but if it doesn't, one has no regrets.

11/05/71

I spent a large part of the day clearing my new movie camera through customs. Barbados is a duty-free port, but the paperwork is difficult when you leave the island on an inter-island freighter and not on a cruise ship or airplane. I turned in my trusty bicycle to the Peace Corps office, with many thanks, and said my good-byes and thanks to all the great people I had met. At five in the afternoon, with my sidekicks Ian and Gregg, I left Barbados on the *People's Choice*.

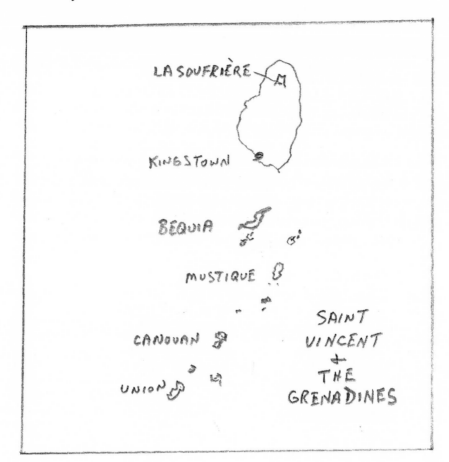

Chapter 9: Saint Vincent and Bequia

We arrived in Saint Vincent around 6:15 the next morning, after a fine one hundred-mile crossing. Our port of entry was Kingstown, the capitol and chief port of the country. This beautiful volcanic island is approximately one hundred and fifty square miles in area, and much of it is too steep for habitation. The slopes also severely restrict the building of roads.

The Ciboney Indians, who had a hunter-gatherer culture, originally inhabited the island. The Arawak Indians, who had a more elaborate farming culture, displaced the Ciboney Indians. The Carib Indians took over the island one hundred years before the first Europeans landed. The warlike nature of the Carib Indians kept outsiders off the island until 1635, and in that year a Dutch slave ship sank near the island and the black slave survivors were allowed to remain there. The slaves and the Indians intermingled, and the result was a group known as the Black Caribs. By 1700 the island population had split, with Yellow Caribs living in the west and the Black Caribs living in the east. These two groups finally let some French live on the island. The British took over in 1783 with the Treaty of Versailles.

There were many conflicts between the Indians and the British. As a result of the second Carib war, the Indians were removed from the island. The Caribs were finally sent to Honduras in ships, where they became known as the Garifuna people. The Garifuna still live in Honduras and Belize as well as in small groups in other parts of the world. To this day, cannons at the forts on Saint Vincent aim inland as well as at the sea as a defense against the Carib Indians.

After the wars, a plantation economy relying on slaves and indentured servants was established. In 1812, the volcano Soufriere erupted and devastated most of the island. Some of the infrastructure was rebuilt, but in 1902 the volcano erupted again, killing over two thousand people. The deaths occurred on the northern end of the island, where most of the remaining Caribs still lived. These eruptions created the lava rock that gives Saint Vincent its beautiful black sand beaches.

In 1969, Saint Vincent became self-governing as an associated state within Great Britain. This was the form of government during my visit. Saint Vincent became fully independent in 1979. Clearing customs in Saint Vincent was a hassle for me since I had no formal exit plan. The island governments are very concerned about people showing up on their shores and never leaving. Ian and Gregg were returning to Barbados on the *People's Choice*, but I was planning to find a different ride north. Customs finally allowed me to enter the country as a passenger on *People's Choice*. If I did not find a ride north and clear it with them, I would have to return to Barbados with Ian and Gregg.

We left Kingstown harbor around two in the afternoon and headed south to Bequia, where the captain lived. The one-and-a-half-hour voyage was through a large thunderstorm, but the weather cleared just as we approached Bequia. The small island appeared out of the gloom like a green jewel. Bequia is only about five miles in length (seven square miles), but its harbor is one of the prettiest in the Caribbean. It is the largest of the Grenadines, and its economy was based on fishing, boatbuilding, and whaling. Whales are in the vicinity of Bequia seasonally. Since some of the earliest Europeans who settled there were whalers, the art of boatbuilding and whaling has remained strong on the island. We slept on the *People's Choice* that night, and I hoped that I could find a boat to take me north the next day.

11/07/71

I went snorkeling off the freighter and caught a fish for dinner. I also saw barracuda and lobster in abundance. My inability to stay underwater for any great length of time really reinforced my desire to learn how to scuba dive when I returned to the United States. I borrowed the dingy from the *People's Choice* and rowed around the harbor, looking for my ride north. My good luck was still with me, and I found the seventy-foot ketch, *Kerynia*, which belonged to a young British couple. Jim and Betty had bought the vintage yacht and planned to sail the islands, chartering during tourist season. Jim had been working on the huge diesel engine, and a valve spring had shot out during replacement, caught his thumb, and dislocated it. His bad luck was my good luck since he had much work left to do and needed help. They were heading north to Antigua to pick up their regular crew and start the charter season.

After I called up to the boat, Jim looked down at me in the dingy and said, "I don't know where you came from, but go get your bag and come aboard!" I rowed back to the freighter as fast as I could. I said my quick good-byes to Ian and Gregg, who were returning to Barbados the next day. They rowed me, and my big bag, back to the *Kerynia*.

11/08/71

The *Kerynia* was a seventy-foot, ketch-rigged (two masts) sailboat. She was built as a luxury yacht with large staterooms and a galley fine for cooking for many guests. There was a huge salon above the engine room for entertaining. She had been commandeered during World War II for use as a minesweeper and then refitted as a yacht after the war. She was very well built and could travel just as well as a sailboat or under power with her huge twelve-cylinder engine. She was in need of some sprucing up before taking on any paying guests, so I was put to work. I did lots of sanding and varnishing, as well as things like diving under her to scrape the propeller.

11/09/71

This day was spent like a true sailor, sanding railings and the eighty-five-foot main mast. I am not sure how Jim managed to winch me up the mast with only one hand, but he did and so the work got done.

I met a nice couple, Pat and Ruth, from South Africa who had just sailed across the Atlantic with their two small boys. They were planning to spend the winter in the Caribbean and then keep on traveling around the world. Pat was a photographer and was doing a film he would call, *The Voyage of the Sandefjord* (the name of their boat). The *Sandefjord* was a double-ender sloop that had circumnavigated the earth at least once before, so they were pretty confident of their chances for success. Their two young boys were amazing on the boat and could do all the tasks asked of them. They could also handle the dingy better than any adult. What a childhood, to travel around the world like that! I believe that National Geographic was going to release the movie when Pat finished it.

11/10/71–11/12/71

A sailor's work is never done, so I continued to sand and varnish. To varnish the eighty-five-foot mainmast, I was hoisted to the top in a boson's chair. As I completed a portion above me, I was lowered a few feet and did some more. After countless repetitions of this sequence, I finally reached the deck.

I neglected to mention that Betty had been a stewardess and a gourmet cook in her former life. After these hard days of refurbishing the boat, we all sat down to some tremendous meals, either on deck or in the big salon. Eventually I sanded and varnished both masts and all the woodwork on *Kerynia*, and we were ready to head north to Saint Lucia for new batteries and valve springs.

11/13/71

I encountered all kinds of characters in those island harbors. On this day I met Jack, who was living on his little boat by himself. He claimed to be a "Shan-go" priest, which is something similar to voodoo. He was British and apparently the black sheep of his family, who sent him a monthly stipend to live on. He seemed to be quite content to sit on the stern of his little boat and meditate most of the day. His family apparently didn't care what he did as long as he stayed in the Caribbean to do it. I didn't want to be a "Shan-go" priest, but the idea of living in the Caribbean on a monthly stipend sure sounded good to me! The island countries don't mind if one stays anchored in their harbors spending money since one is living on one's way to another location. If people make trouble, however, the authorities just send the offender on their way in their own boat and tell them not to return.

11/14/71

I took a day off work and went diving with Pat and Jim. Most of the people anchored in the harbor would either fish from their boats or go spear fishing to get something for the dinner table. We were successful, and Betty cooked up a fine meal as usual. One could get used to living like this.

11/15/71–11/16/71

More work to get the boat in condition for paying guests. Life on a sailboat is wonderful, but the work of keeping a boat shipshape never ends. To keep a charter yacht up to the standards of paying guests requires a lot more maintenance than just day-to-day quality. People pay a lot for an island getaway and usually expect pretty high standards. I discovered that there were indeed different levels or standards of charter sailboats with corresponding price levels. The *Kerynia* was being marketed to the upper crust of the market and her standards were very high.

11/17/71

We finally weighed anchor and left the Bequia harbor. We headed north to Kingstown, Saint Vincent. Since we were sailing at about six knots, the trip took one and a half hours. *Kerynia* could achieve at least that speed under power, but fuel costs money and why not sail a sailboat whenever possible?

We had tied up to the wharf in Bequia before we headed north to fill up our water tank. It was both cheaper and easier to do this in a smaller port. The water was no doubt fresher and cleaner there also. While waiting for the tank to fill, I slipped over the side to do a little snorkeling and check the rudder. The stone wall that made up the wharf was pockmarked with lots of holes, and each one was home to some critter. Down at about ten feet, I was looking around at the inhabitants. When I turned around, I was face to face with a green moray eel whose head was bigger than mine! Morays have very poor eyesight and can be territorial. I was only snorkeling, not scuba diving, and had been down a minute already. I let out what air I still had in me from shock, and luckily the eel did not take action and I was able to return to the surface. A moray's teeth are quite large and curved inward for gripping. Even if the eel does not want to eat its victim, it is very difficult to get out of its grip if bitten by one. The harder that one pulls away from a moray, the deeper in their teeth sink. They also lock their tail section into their hole so that pulling them out and up is not an option. I have no idea how long the eel was, but I'm sure glad that it did not strike across the six inches separating our faces! This was another time when I really wished that I could scuba dive instead of just snorkeling. With a tank of air, I could have backed off and enjoyed the experience of seeing one of these amazing creatures and not been so intimidated. I have encountered many morays since that day and have never had a bad experience. They are scary at first sight but not too dangerous if given some space.

11/18/71

We left our mooring in Kingstown around six in the morning, trying to get an early start for our trip north to Saint Lucia. I had cleared customs the day before with Jim and Betty since I now had a valid means of transportation. We arrived in the port of Castries at three-thirty in the afternoon after a good trip. *Kerynia* had made around six knots during the trip, which was quite decent for a boat of her size in a light wind. The coasts of Saint Vincent and Saint Lucia are spectacular. They are both wonderful examples of volcanic islands, and they stick right out of the blue Caribbean Sea. My movies from the trip show off their grandeur but really shock the audience when I zoom in on sixty or seventy-foot sailboats anchored near shore. The boats appear as small specks against the towering vertical faces of the volcanic peaks. The movie *Pirates of the Caribbean* was filmed on the coast of Saint Vincent, and it represents that perfect island atmosphere. The pirates may not have been as kind as portrayed in the film, but they sure had a nice backyard to play in!

Chapter 10: Saint Lucia

Saint Lucia is approximately twenty-seven by fourteen miles (238 square miles), and its most distinguishing features are the twin volcanic peaks referred to as the Pitons. They rise directly out of the sea to up over two thousand feet and are really impressive from the deck of a seventy-foot boat. In the interior of the island is a rainforest, which is now a national park. Thank goodness countries are protecting their natural wonders. Tourism is a great way to boost an economy, if there is something to show the tourists. Another unique feature is Saint Lucia's Mount Soufriere, which is billed as the world's only drive-in volcano. One can get to its interior by car and see the sulfur springs there. Due to its verticality, Saint Lucia has few roads. The sightseeing is worth the trip to the places that are accessible.

I spent the first day in Saint Lucia cutting and attaching lines for a new awning that Jim and Betty had bought. They felt that they needed to provide shade for their guests when they were not en route between islands. We cleared customs upon arrival in Castries, as we had to check in at our first port of arrival in each of these island nations and then check out as we left for the next island. As long as visitors have their own transportation and money to pay for goods and services ashore, they are very welcome.

11/20/71

The awning was finally completed, so we all went ashore to do some sightseeing. I went up to Coleman Hill's house. I had no money to hire a car, so my touring was limited to walking around the town of Castries.

11/21/71

I spent the day bumming around and settled on a new career as a floating Mr. Fix-it. I could live in the harbors and lend assistance to yachts from my floating workshop. It was a great idea, if only I had a boat large enough to house my workshop and me. I did eventually become a building contractor on an island, but it was on land building houses. As a twenty-four-year-old vagabond I had lots of time to ponder my future, and it's interesting how much this thinking influenced my lifestyle in future years.

11/22/71

There was no work that had to be accomplished this day, so I went ashore again and met Sid Patterson. He had trained with my brother in the Peace Corps, and in fact he was the volunteer who had stayed with Miss Bryan in Trinidad. I went up to his house for dinner and ended up staying overnight due to a bad rainstorm. Sid's lifestyle as a volunteer on Saint Lucia was better than we had experienced in Brasil but less ostentatious than that of the volunteers on Barbados. I wish that I had had the opportunity to see more of the interior of Saint Lucia, but Sid did not have access to personal transportation. Hiring a car to take me around, like I said before, was outside my budget. My other problem was that I was still a member of the *Kerynia* crew and expected back on board to work for my room and board.

11/23/71–11/25/71

I returned to the boat in the morning, did some painting, and ran some errands for Jim. At this time I was becoming aware of a growing rift between Betty and me. She had apparently gotten tired of having a twenty-four-year-old "Yank" living on her boat and maybe taking up too much of her husband's time. Jim and I got along fine, and it was a lot easier getting the boat ready for tourist season with two sets of hands. I had grown up around boats and also loved to tinker with engines. I may not have been an expert at any of the jobs, but I fell like I was a pretty competent crewman. Also, my only wages were room and board, not much of an overhead for them. But as I mentioned before, they were a young couple in a foreign environment, and I think Betty wanted to have a larger chunk of Jim's time and attention to herself. Until they started having guests aboard, she would have little company except for Jim. She apparently wanted a younger, "native" crew, who would take orders and then disappear when not needed. The next day she found a guy who fit that description and he came aboard. He acted as if he had won the lottery and ran around like he owned the boat. He would take the dingy to run errands and then stay out cruising around the harbor, showing off to his friends. I think Jim had an idea as to how this was going to work out for him, but he didn't want to fight with Betty over it.

I continued to do my chores and watch our new cabin boy goof off. Practically anything that I said with my "Yank" accent irritated Betty. I had a feeling during these days that things might not last too long for me.

11/26/71

I had my final round with Betty and left the boat looking for Sid. I found him and returned to the boat for my bag. I said good-bye to Jim, who did not want me to go but did not want to fight with his wife either. Since I now had no transportation off the island, I was forced to buy an airline ticket to Miami for over one hundred dollars. I could not stay on the island without a way off, and this was my only option at the time.

While I was resolving this problem with customs, I ran into another boat owner, Teak. He owned the sixty-foot sloop *Jonathan Swift*. Teak was an acquaintance of Jim and Betty and took pity on my situation. He said, "Get your bag from customs, and you can go on my boat. I'm heading out for Antigua tomorrow and you are welcome to come along." He was heading north to start the charter season also and only had one crewman and a friend on board. That left plenty of room for me on the boat, and once again my luck was with me. I went back and explained everything to customs, and they let me turn in my airplane ticket. I had one other way off the island at the time, which was to book passage on the inter-island federal mail boat. That boat was not due to arrive for at least a week, and the customs officer didn't want me hanging around that long.

11/27/71

By going with Teak, I was ahead of the schedule that Jim and Betty had for arriving in Antigua. We planned to sail straight through, which involved sailing all day and then all night as well. The four of us took turns at the wheel. Life on *Jonathan Swift* was much different than on *Kerynia*. It was just four guys on the open sea on a sixty-foot boat. She was not a luxury yacht by any stretch, but she had all the necessary accoutrements to make her livable. The *Jonathan Swift* felt more like a sailboat to me than the much larger boat I had been on for the past several weeks. She was also a lot faster. Instead of gourmet cooking, we dined on a huge pot of spaghetti that could be reheated as needed. There was plenty of ice-cold beer and coffee to drink by the gallon at night.

After dinner we talked for quite some time about life in the Caribbean until finally Teak said, "I've had it, and I'm going to get some sleep."

His friend Ted replied," Me too, see you in the morning."

That left Teak's only real crewmember and me. He told me that we could take turns navigating, and I said," Just bring me coffee from time to time and make sure that I'm still awake." I had the privilege of sailing the boat most of that night, steering by the stars. Navigating this way involves steering the boat onto a course by way of a compass and then lining up the mast with a star. Since the stars are shifting constantly, I had to realign with a new star from time to time, but it beat looking at a compass for hours on end. Sailing by the stars on a gorgeous Caribbean night is one of the best experiences that I could wish for.

Teak's crewman checked on me from time to time as promised, and I made it through the night without hitting an island or anything else, for that matter. During the day, we had passed many small, dugout canoes with outboard motors. How these fishermen got around in these boats, miles from anywhere, beats the heck out of me. We also saw quite a number of other sailboats, both nearby and on the horizon. I had worried about running into one of these boats at night, but none passed very close that night.

Having had the chance to sail on these charter sailboats in the Caribbean definitely explained to me why so many people are lured to rent a yacht for a week or so for the experience. I don't know if I could live on one of these boats full time, but part time is heaven. And Jimmy Buffet says it best—"Changes in latitude, changes in attitude."

CODRINGTON

BARBUDA

SAINT
JOHN'S

ANTIGUA

ENGLISH
HARBOUR

Chapter 11: Antigua

We finally arrived in Antigua at around three-thirty in the afternoon after twenty-eight and a half hours. We had a great trip, and I was much closer to the United States. The island lies at seventeen degrees north latitude, only seventeen degrees south of Key West, Florida. Antigua is an island of 108 square miles (114 miles by 11 miles), and it is not as rugged as the islands further south. We arrived at English Harbor on the south coast. Admiral Horatio Nelson established the harbor in 1784 to control shipping in the neighboring parts of the Caribbean. The harbor was so well laid out that little has changed to this day. It now serves as one of the most popular yachting harbors for Caribbean cruising.

After a similar history of Indian occupation as the other islands, the first Europeans arrived in Antigua around 1684. Christopher Codrington started sugar plantations, which eventually numbered one hundred or so. Each plantation had a windmill for grinding the cane. The stone towers of the mills still stand, and some of the mills have been restored. These restored mills serve as bars, restaurants, and even houses. Most of the population is descended from slaves who worked the plantations and were eventually officially freed in 1834. Antigua became an associated state in 1967 (the type of government during my trip) and received full independence from Great Britain in 1981.

After clearing customs once again, I went to Ted Starns's house. Ted was the other non-crew on the *Jonathan Swift* and one of Teak's friends. Again, my good fortune in meeting these interesting people led me to an insight into life on the islands that I never would have had just traveling alone as a regular tourist. Ted lived on Antigua since he worked for a big oil company with interests there. In his backyard he was constructing a fifty-foot catamaran out of plywood. The craft looked huge out of water and I asked Ted, "How are you ever going to get her into the water when you finish construction?"

He replied, "My company has several large derricks that we use to move around equipment at the yard. When I have the hull finished, they will lend me one to carry her to a suitable launching spot." His house was approximately half a mile from the shoreline, so I guess the trip was possible. It would have been a sight to witness the launching. I had watched several twenty-foot fishing boats being launched in Brasil, but this catamaran was huge in comparison. The smaller fishing boats were mounted on wooden-wheeled carts. They were then pushed and pulled by as many as twenty volunteers. The route from the boat builders shed to the water was mostly over smooth rock, so the trip was not too difficult. If the boats had to be turned, half the volunteers just lifted one end of the vessel and moved it over a little. Eventually the rocky bank of the river allowed the boat to roll downhill and several ropes tied to the boat controlled its progress. Ted's huge catamaran could never have been launched in this manner. We had time for a brief tour, and I spent the night at Ted's house.

Chapter 12: Puerto Rico

11/29/71

In the morning, Ted took me to the airport, where I caught the 9:05 AM flight to San Juan, Puerto Rico. The great flight over the jewel-like islands below arrived around ten. I had been accustomed to seeing the islands from the perspective of a boat deck, and this new view gave me a greater appreciation for how lovely these dots in the blue-green sea really were. Christopher Columbus and his crew must have thought they had died and gone to heaven when they first sighted these islands. Having not seen land for so long, they were desperate, but this sight would still have been a little overwhelming.

I was finally back in the United States! The answer to the question that you have had since the first paragraph will now be revealed. I had to clear customs once again, after nearly a dozen times during the past three months. This time, however, I was entering my own country. My appearance was a bit scruffy by this time, but I had bathed at Ted's house. I was therefore a little more presentable than I would have been straight off Teak's boat, for example. I had on my cleanest clothes, though they had not seen the inside of a washing machine for some time. Still, they weren't that bad.

The woman at the customs desk was just trying to do her job, I guess, but she sure ended up with a large pile of garbage on her table. By the time my bag was nearly empty, her table had no room left on it. I guess that the phenomenal luck, which had carried me so far, had not run completely out. With only two pairs of dirty socks left in the bag, she ended the game and told me, "Put everything back in that bag and get out of here!" The knife and the disassembled twenty-two-caliber pistol made it through one last customs check and I was home free. I checked my big bag into a locker at the airport since I did not want to carry it around San Juan. I purchased a ticket on the 10:30 AM flight to Miami leaving the next day.

With only my camera, I took a bus into the historic city. I spent the day seeing the ruins at El Morro and walking around the city. I wanted to stay longer, but I was only a few hundred miles from the mainland and I longed to be back. I vowed at the time to return for a longer visit, and I have made good on that promise several times. Few Americans visit this jewel of a place and most forget that it is part of the United States. No passports or visas are necessary for a visit, and one can get a real taste of the Caribbean after only a short hop from Miami. What some people refer to as our 51st state is well worth the visit.

I was longing to hear good old American English again after more than two years. In the streets of San Juan at that time, mostly Spanish was spoken. Today, almost everyone speaks English, even if they use it as a second language. I slept in the airport that night in order to make my early flight.

Chapter 13: The United States

11/30/71

I caught the 10:30 AM flight to Miami. I had hoped to fly on one of the new 747s that I had been watching take off and land in San Juan, but alas, I got a smaller plane and the flight was much like the others of the last month. For someone who had never flown before I went to Peace Corps training in Atlanta, I was becoming very matter of fact about jumping on and off of planes. Flying, in those days, was a pretty simple affair if you had the price of a ticket. The customs in airports were much easier to go through than the ones encountered during land travel. If one traveled on domestic flights within a country, the fares were usually very reasonable. Each country wanted to have its flag on the tail of an airplane, so they subsidized the airlines, making the fares lower.

After retrieving my trusty duffel bag from customs for the last time, I caught a bus to West Palm Beach, Florida. My brother was living there at the time. Upon arrival at his apartment building, I really shocked his friends. My brother is my identical twin, and they were not expecting to see him walk in with a beard and carrying a large bag. My brother was also quite surprised since during my travels I had no way of letting him know where I was or when I would be arriving. We did not have cell phones in those days or even reliable phone service to the places where I had been. My brother and I had a great time catching up after a two-year stretch of only corresponding by mail. I took over his vacant second bedroom and made plans for the rest of my life.

Epilogue

It has been over thirty-seven years since as a twenty-four-year-old kid I made the journey detailed in this book. At that age I thought I knew a lot more than I truly did. If I had known then what I know now, I may never even have attempted the trip. Maturity makes us weigh the consequences of our actions before we undertake projects and may prohibit us from taking some irreplaceable steps. I am very glad that I was so naïve back then and undertook the adventure. Now that I have lived more than twice as long, I wish that I had taken more trips like this one.

Something always comes up as a reason to put off great plans and schemes in life. Eventually one wakes up and finds that one never got to all the places one wanted to go to. Or worse yet, one is too old or broke to go even if one wanted to. I have done lots of exciting things in my life and been to many wonderful places around the world, but there are always those never-gotten-to places that haunt me. This journey proved to me that I could travel with very little planning. By changing even those meager plans, I could enhance the trip. Going with the flow is, I believe, the best way to travel. This method allowed me to interact with the circumstances encountered and the people I met along the way. My wife and I traveled extensively and tried to get advice from everyone we met as to where we should go next and what we should do when we got there. Many of the best locations, campsites, kayaking areas, and hiking trails that we experienced were found from interactions with the people we met while traveling. The best thing is to not plan too much and just get out there and enjoy the journey.

Upon reading through my story, I find that I sound a bit bitter at times about the disparity between the Peace Corps life in Brasil and in some other countries. I want to make it clear that my Peace Corps experience was the best one I have ever had and I would not change a thing. A large part of the whole concept of the Peace Corps, as set up by Sargent Shriver (JFK established the Peace Corps and LBJ kept it funded, but Shriver was the one who designed it and made it work), was to expose Americans to other cultures. By living in a manner close to that of the people we were sent to help, we matured and gained a perspective of the world that very few opinionated, uninformed Americans will ever have. The lifestyle and media coverage in the United States gives a very poor view of how the world really is. By seeing the United States from the outside, one can better view how we really are and how the rest of the world sees us. The planet is shrinking, and we all need to get along.

I have lived my life in a much different way than I ever would have if I had not spent two years of it in Brasil, working with the Peace Corps. I learned to listen better (when one cannot understand the language, one had better listen better), and I learned to respect other points of view since I was now in the minority. The countries that have been served by the Peace Corps benefited a lot (we established fishing cooperatives in Brasil that really helped the fishermen), but the United States benefited more by having dramatically changed people come back home with new ideas and opinions.

I doubt that the journey I took in 1971 would be possible today. There is more real danger in going to some of the locations, than there may have been when I did it. The cost would be quite a bit higher now, even if many of the hotels or means of transportation still exist. The landmarks are still there, and I highly recommend seeing as many as possible. The Caribbean is unbelievable and should be visited at least once by everyone.

I am sorry that I lost touch with many of the people I met, traveled with, and who helped me on my journey. The people one meets while traveling, as I have said earlier, are more important than travel agents or knowledge gleaned from the Internet. I hope that everyone who was traveling with me got to his or her destinations as I did. I also hope that they had as great an adventure as well. Finally, I am glad that I kept a pretty good journal so that after all this time I could get the whole story down on paper.

If you haven't been on your journey yet, plan a little and get out there!

About the Author

Brian D. Wyllie is a former Peace Corps volunteer now living in Florida. He became an avid traveler after the experiences covered in the book and has visited many countries around the world. He continues to explore his subtropical home, often by kayak, and travels the world when possible.